terrain

THE CONTAINER GARDEN BOOK

ALSO AVAILABLE

Terrain: Ideas and Inspiration for Decorating the Home and Garden

Terrain: The Houseplant Book: An Insider's Guide to Cultivating and Collecting the Most Sought-After Specimens

terrain

THE CONTAINER GARDEN BOOK

Creative Designs for Every Season

Melissa Bartley & Greg Lehmkuhl

Words by Melissa Bartley & Megan Parry

Principal Photography by Martha Lawlor

ARTISAN | NEW YORK

Library of Congress Cataloging-in-Publication Data is on file.

ISBN 978-1-64829-091-6 (hardcover)
ISBN 978-1-64829-568-3 (ebook)

Design by Becky Terhune

Artisan books may be purchased in bulk for business, educational, or promotional use. For information, please contact your local bookseller or the Hachette Book Group Special Markets Department at special.markets@hbgusa.com.

The publisher is not responsible for websites (or their content) that are not owned by the publisher.

The Hachette Speakers Bureau provides a wide range of authors for speaking events. To find out more, go to hachettespeakersbureau.com or email HachetteSpeakers@hbgusa.com.

Published by Artisan,
an imprint of Workman Publishing,
a division of Hachette Book Group, Inc.
1290 Avenue of the Americas
New York, NY 10104
artisanbooks.com

Printed in China (TLF) on responsibly sourced paper

First printing, March 2026

10 9 8 7 6 5 4 3 2 1

terrain

Contents

INTRODUCTION

In 2008, we opened the doors of our flagship location in Glen Mills, Pennsylvania, on the site of the historic J. Franklin Styer's Nurseries. Our founder, Dick Hayne, having just rekindled a friendship with his own garden but lacking a local source of inspiration, set about gathering a group of like-minded plant, home, and design enthusiasts who would soon become the first Terrain employees. Together, with a lot of hard work and infinite stores of talent, these folks reimagined a garden center with a fresh approach. It's a space devoted to nature, rooted in the seasons, and curated for the garden and home—one that engages all the senses for a wholly immersive experience.

This experiential approach is still the driving force behind everything we do. Every season, our teams dream up and execute displays, installations, and product offerings that celebrate that particular period's special alchemy. We draw inspiration from nature and its rhythms, asking ourselves what we cherish most about each season and how we can weave those elements into our surroundings. What aspects of the changing seasons do we wish to highlight, and what brings us the greatest joy and excitement at home and in the garden? And how do we bring that excitement into our stores?

For us, that starts with our container designs. Our planters greet you the minute you set foot on the grounds of one of our stores—a prelude to the creativity to come. We see container gardens as an invitation to experiment, to ditch the "set it and forget it" philosophy and open ourselves up to play. Every empty planter is a potential fantasyland where self-expression is thoughtfully tended and prescribed garden rules are put to bed. Container gardens are an opportunity to embrace the ephemeral and honor the fleeting beauty of the natural world. They offer freedom to indulge in your most unconventional design ideas, whether you're spotlighting exceptional specimens that would otherwise struggle in a garden bed or pairing an unusual mix of plants in the same soil.

After years of working side by side with our incredible store teams, lifetimes of experimenting in our own gardens, and learning from our communities of curious gardeners from California to Connecticut, we thought it was time to bring together our most outrageous inspiration, guiding principles, and styling philosophies we use for every container we plant—both for Terrain and own personal enjoyment.

In keeping with our nature-first ethos, we've organized this book by the four seasons, and each chapter offers specific plant and design ideas that align with the natural beauty and resources of that time of year. Throughout, you'll find practical advice on container silhouettes, materials, drainage, soil mixes, and more to support healthy growth. And, of course, you'll find vibrant planters captured by immersive photography that illustrates our signature naturalistic, perfectly imperfect style and showcases how container gardens can fit anywhere, from petite urban patios to sprawling rural backyards.

The allure in container gardening lies in its potential for reinvention. Every season, you have an opportunity to repeat what works and tweak what doesn't. Where you start is not where you'll end up. We wrote this book in the hope that it will find a permanent place on your potting table, soil streaked and oft consulted, a jumping-off point as you create your own natural wonderlands. If you're willing to get your hands dirty and go for it, you're already on your way.

terrain

OUR APPROACH TO CONTAINER PLANTING

Whether you're a nascent green thumb with a sliver of a balcony on a high-rise building or a seasoned gardener with an expansive-but-bare backyard, you have the power to transform your space with an array of colors, plant types, themes, and placements. You can use the ideas on the pages that follow no matter where you are in your gardening journey or where you live. Just let your creativity lead the way. Maybe you'll turn your patio into a Mediterranean retreat with olive trees, lemon trees, lavender, and rosemary one year, and a tropical paradise vibrant with pink bougainvillea and silver Bismarck palms the next.

Design Principles

Thriller, filler, spiller. It's a well-trod planter design technique, and for good reason. The simple rule—adding one standout plant, one easily massed plant, and one trailing specimen—is an effective way to get a balanced, pleasing combination every time. But we believe every rule is meant to be broken. Instead, we look to the art world for inspiration. How do painters find balance within a canvas? Where do ceramicists find dynamism within a sculpture? Containers themselves are living artworks, and we've reinterpreted the following art school design principles for our plantings.

RHYTHM

Rhythm is what guides the viewer's eye, inviting it to dance across the composition by providing both movement and moments of rest. In the Queen of the Autumn Garden (shown opposite; see more on page 180), rhythm is established by the strong vertical arrangement of deep red 'Arabian Night' dahlias. Their dark, velvety blooms punctuate the planter like a syncopated beat, pulling the gaze upward. Beneath this canopy, the swaying tufts of little bluestem echo the vertical rhythm, creating continuity through color, movement, and form. Amaranth unfurls in smoky purple tendrils, creating a natural sequence of lift, pause, and flow. The eye rises with the dahlias, rests in the cool greens of their foliage, then drifts down again, completing the visual cycle. A successful design embraces contrast while maintaining cohesion—echoing the natural rhythm found in nature.

EMPHASIS

The use of a strong focal point—typically, one or two standout features—anchors a composition and provides structure. A dominant element also serves as the foundation around which supporting plants are arranged, creating a

hierarchy in the planting. Anything can be an emphasized feature: a bold plant, driftwood or branches, a special container, or even negative space. In the fall container Harvest Moon (shown above; see more on page 160), spheres dominate the design. The planter itself is round, as are the pumpkins, and the cabbages echo the spherical dance that is happening. Emphasis ensures that even in a highly diverse planting scheme, there is always a clear point of reference that ties the composition together.

UNITY

There should be an underlying thread—be it color, form, texture, or structure—that weaves a planted design together to create a harmonious whole. Color is one of the most powerful unifying tools in design, capable of linking diverse plant selections. In Blue Skies (shown below; see more on page 118), a restrained palette of soft blues and greens ties the planting together. The powder blue patina of the sculptural branch harmonizes with the cape plumbago blooms and cool-toned foliage, creating subtle color continuity. Equally important is the unity of form: The twisting branch mirrors the shape and movement of the rosemary, blurring the line between plant and object. The sleek gray planter grounds the design without distracting, blending with the surrounding stone. Without these unifying threads, the arrangement might feel messy or disparate, but instead Blue Skies becomes a harmonious and quietly expressive whole.

BALANCE

Balance refers to the distribution of visual weight: how the elements in a container interact to create a sense of stability or movement. This doesn't mean the planting has to be literally symmetrical—in fact, some of our favorite planting designs rely on off-center plants or pockets of empty space to achieve their own kind of balance. For example, in a naturalistic border, balance might be achieved by offsetting the weight of tall, airy 'Karl Foerster' feather reed grass on one side with a cluster of sturdy, rounded coneflower on the other. In Purple Majesty (shown above; see more on page 149), the tall, airy little bluestem is placed off-center and balanced by the dense aster, as if trying to ensure the container doesn't visually "tip over."

PROPORTION

While plant sizes should generally be chosen to complement the size of the container, intentional shifts in scale can create striking visual effects. A well-proportioned planting considers not just the vessel but also the broader setting—what feels balanced in an intimate courtyard might be lost in a vast landscape. A powerful example of proportion used for dramatic impact is the Bonsai Light Cascade (shown below; see more on page 211). This holiday container features a 42-inch-wide (107 cm) low bowl planter, dramatically contrasted by a 9-foot-tall (2.7 m) weeping white pine with an expansive, undulating form. The exaggerated height adds a sense of movement, while winter lighting transforms the display into a glowing focal point in the landscape. Playful, dynamic, and unexpected, this design demonstrates how proportion can be deliberately manipulated to create visual intrigue and presence.

CONTRAST

The counterbalance to unity, contrast emphasizes differences in color, form, and texture, distinguishing individual elements to create a dynamic composition. Without contrast, a design can feel monotonous; too much contrast, however, can feel chaotic. The key is to strike a balance—using contrast to highlight focal points while maintaining cohesion within the broader design. One of our favorite ways to introduce contrast is to play with texture. In Desert Meadow Harmony (shown above; see more on page 104), the colors of the plants are very similar—cool gray greens and soft blue flowers. The architectural shape of the aloe is a beautiful contrast to the soft foliar texture of the variegated blue daisy. The result is a planting with a layered, tactile quality that invites closer inspection.

Plant Types

Each time we visit a nursery, we fill our cart with a diverse array of plants, imagining the possibilities ahead before bringing them home. The plants you find at your local garden center will vary based on your geographic location, what is considered an annual and a perennial in your region, and seasonality. The following plant types are the ones you'll see most commonly in the pages of this book, but we encourage you to be open to surprises when you're shopping.

TREES AND SHRUBS

Planting trees and shrubs in containers can set them apart from the surrounding landscape, drawing the viewer's eye to these singular plants' noteworthy qualities. This approach works well for both large-scale trees and shrubs as well as smaller specimens with especially interesting scents or blooms. Trees also offer year-round appeal: Evergreens give a verdant flash no matter the season, and even if they have no blooms or leaves, deciduous tree branches (like those of the 'Helen Everitt' rhododendron shown below) can make a sculptural statement.

ANNUALS

Annuals' transient nature—given that they last just a single growing season—invites bold experimentation with new color palettes, textures, plant groupings, and spatial arrangements. Vibrant coleus, shown below, are a favorite, as they perform well up until frost. This ability to transform spaces for a single season means annuals are perfect for marking special events or showcasing trending garden styles.

PERENNIALS

One of the key benefits of perennials in container gardening is that their longevity means they can serve as a reliable "anchor" to support and balance an ever-changing cast of seasonal grasses and annuals. Whether it's the architectural height of foxtail lilies or the leafy backdrop of hardy foliage plants like hostas or ferns, perennials establish a visual rhythm that can be refreshed with minimal effort. Their adaptability allows gardeners to update containers throughout the year by incorporating new accents—such as vibrant blooms in spring, airy grasses in summer, or textural evergreens in winter. Below, a favorite group of perennial pollinators that give high visual interest from summer into fall and leave incredible seed heads for wintering birds: echinacea, rudbeckia, and echibeckia.

SUCCULENTS

Succulents' unusual growing patterns, broad-spectrum color shading, and sculptural shapes make them a fun and unexpected addition to a container planting of perennials and annuals; low-growing varieties in particular can be used to add a secondary layer of intrigue. A 'Quicksilver' kalanchoe, for example, serves as a gorgeous silver-blue understory in the planter below. Unlike cacti, for which they are sometimes mistaken, succulents can tolerate some moisture and do quite well in a mixed container, as long as it doesn't get waterlogged. They're a hardy, drought-resistant, and low-maintenance choice.

ORNAMENTAL GRASSES

Like succulents, ornamental grasses (like the purple love grass shown below) are sturdy and low maintenance. They provide year-round interest in a container planting, maintaining impactful texture and movement from spring through winter. This quality—along with their notorious height—makes them a robust choice for adding easy romance to containers. We especially love pairing naturalistic grasses with polished vessels and traditional annuals like ornamental peppers and coleus to create an interesting high-low effect.

Planting Formulas

While you can, of course, add any variety, color, or texture to any planter you choose, we find that the following formulas are foolproof starting points that deliver aesthetically pleasing and creatively interesting results every time.

SINGLE-VARIETY PLANTINGS

Imagine a lush mound of lavender, vertical spires of ornamental grasses, a cluster of vibrant tulips, or a large, sculptural agave. Single-variety planters embody the beauty of simplicity and boldness, celebrating the unique qualities of a single plant species. At Terrain, we value how this approach allows a plant's texture, color, and form to have its moment without distraction, showcasing its natural elegance. This style is particularly effective for plants with dramatic features and creates a streamlined look that complements both traditional and modern spaces. Agave Eden (page 185) is a great example of an architectural specimen boldly standing out in a planter placed in the wild garden.

MONOCHROME PLANTINGS

By focusing on a single shade range (maybe your planter is red, but you're including hues from scarlet to magenta), you can create a cohesive and sophisticated look with minimal effort. This approach allows the subtle variations in texture, shape, and tone within the chosen color family to truly shine, offering depth and interest without overwhelming the eye. This is a formula you'll see us use over and over again in the pages of this book. All Fired Up (page 111) uses monochromatic plants in blazing hues across a range of plant material. The color is strong and playful, effectively pulling the eye across the various corals, pinks, oranges, and reds but reading as a unified color.

TEXTURAL PLANTINGS

By combining plants with varying leaf shapes, sizes, and finishes—such as the glossy sheen of ivy, the velvety softness of lamb's ear, and the feathery lightness of grasses—you can craft a planter that invites closer inspection. Textural contrast is also enhanced by mixing upright, mounding, and trailing plants, giving the arrangement structure and movement and considering how the plants work off the texture of the planter itself. They are perfect for gardeners who want arrangements that feel layered. Chameleon Fade (shown opposite; see more on page 193) subtly plays with the varying textures of stonecrop, millet, coleus, silver tree plant, bronze fennel, and aged hydrangea, showing that you don't have to rely on flowers to create an artful planter.

CONTAINER MASSING

Grouping containers of varying sizes, shapes, and heights creates visual layers to your landscape and can be used to add depth to garden corners, frame entryways, define outdoor living spaces (like back porches), and serve as dramatic focal points. Use complementary container materials or a unified plant palette for a cohesive display, like we did with Tulip Terrace (page 50). There, the design's impact comes from the sheer number of planters present. The tulips, in their sherbet rainbow, blend to create a single grouping.

Container Placement

Where you decide to place your planter will have a big effect on its overall visual impact. In the planting opposite (see more on page 114), the container is placed just outside the garden, extending the reach of the garden into the gravel pathway. Situating a low bowl full of grasses at the edge of a wildflower garden will have a much different result than placing that same container at the start of a wide driveway. Do you want your planter to blend into its surroundings or stand out? Is it meant to be enjoyed up close and in the round, or at a distance, from only one angle? We're sharing a few of our favorite areas to arrange planters here.

PORCHES AND ENTRYWAYS

Create an inviting first impression by placing containers on porches or flanking entryways.

- Frame doors or steps with seasonal blooms, lush foliage, or elegant evergreens.
- Use tiered arrangements for depth and tall containers for structure.
- Enhance the sensory experience with fragrant plants or cascading greenery.

INDOOR AND OUTDOOR LIVING SPACES

Use containers to define zones indoors or soften patios and decks outdoors.

- Place greenery near seating areas or use cascading plants on shelves for vertical interest.
- Strategically position containers to unify indoor-outdoor flow and connect spaces.

UNTAPPED CORNERS

Transform underused corners with bold statement planters or layered arrangements.

- Outdoors, soften corners with cascading foliage or tall architectural plants.
- Add a sense of discovery by placing eye-catching planters in a faraway corner.

WINDOW BOXES AND WALLS

Add charm and color with window boxes filled with trailing plants, blooms, or herbs.

- Use wall-mounted planters or living walls to maximize space and create lush features.
- Experiment with cascading greenery or structured patterns for visual impact.

AT THE GARDEN'S EDGE

Place containers at the edge of gardens to transition between structured and natural landscapes.

- Frame the garden with contrasting plant forms and textures.
- Update seasonally to highlight specific blooms or foliage while maintaining flexibility.

ARCHITECTURAL PUNCTUATION

Use containers as bold focal points to add structure and rhythm to spaces.

- Anchor key areas like patio corners, pathway ends, or garden entry points.
- Choose striking shapes or tall plants to draw the eye and enhance vertical interest.

TABLETOP

Place compact containers on dining, coffee, or side tables for a natural touch.

- Use low-growing or cascading plants to keep views clear and arrangements neat.
- Seasonal blooms, succulents, or herbs make versatile and functional centerpieces.

SPRING

As nature wakes up once again, we celebrate a return to the garden with a sense of renewed creativity. After a long winter, there's nothing better than diving hands first into the soil and bringing fresh ideas to life. Containers are the perfect canvas to unleash all those visions dreamed up during the colder months.

Now is the time to test new varieties, play with color palettes, and explore how different textures combine. Early-season favorites, such as bulbs and cool-weather annuals, thrive in containers and can be easily updated as the season progresses. By midseason, you'll see the results of your efforts taking shape, and by summer, the once modest plants will be thriving centerpieces. This narrative of growth and change is what makes spring planting such a meaningful and transformative experience for gardeners. Each plant is a living canvas, offering surprises as it matures—a burst of unexpected color, a new layer of texture, or the way it interacts with neighboring plants in a container.

Spring Color Inspiration

We love celebrating delicate pastel hues during spring. These light colors are just as striking as their bolder summer counterparts—there's strength in their nascent softness.

Emerging Green

Capture the energy of spring with a vibrant yet soothing combination of colors that brings a sense of renewal and vitality.

Euphorbia epithymoides **'Golden Fusion'**
(cushion spurge)

Helleborus foetidus **'Wester Flisk'**
(stinking hellebore)

Nassella tenuissima **'Pony Tails'**
(feather grass)

Helleborus argutifolius
(Corsican hellebore)

Hydrangea paniculata **'Jane'**
(aka Little Lime) (panicle hydrangea)

Petunia **'Keiyeul'** (aka Surfinia Lime)
(petunia)

Tulipa **'Sweet Light'** (tulip)

Leucobryum glaucum (cushion moss)

Hydrangea macrophylla **'Horwack'**
(aka Pistachio) (bigleaf hydrangea)

Terra-Cotta Blush

Embody the gentle warmth of spring with a harmonious palette of muted tones that evokes the quiet elegance of the season.

Narcissus 'Spring Pride' (daffodil)

Viburnum carlesii (Korean spice viburnum)

Graptopetalum paraguayense (ghost plant)

Cercis canadensis 'Ncec1' (aka Carolina Sweetheart) (eastern redbud)

Carex buchananii 'Red Rooster' (sedge)

Cydonia oblonga 'Meech's Prolific' (quince)

Astrantia major (masterwort)

Heuchera 'Beauty Color' (coralbells)

Foeniculum vulgare 'Purpureum' (bronze fennel)

Nested in Nature

Our own offering to Eostre, the Germanic goddess of spring, this nature-inspired "Easter basket" embodies the hope and growth that we celebrate during the equinox, with nary a plastic egg or jelly bean in sight. The hyacinths burst forth all at once, the intoxicating fragrance heralding their arrival, and just as quickly will be spent. A foraged bird's nest reminds us of new beginnings. Our planter is a welcome exclamation as a table centerpiece or a naturalistic "outcropping" placed on a weathered tree stump in the yard.

Planted in abundance, the purple hyacinths topple over each other and the curves of the container, creating a strong directional composition that allows the eye to wander peacefully around the planting. The natural textures and tones of the dried ostrich fern fronds that we plucked from the garden create a pleasing juxtaposition to those vibrant flowers and match the color of the aged planter. (Dried fern fronds are easy to find at most craft stores or online retailers like Etsy.)

The undulating silhouette of this planter mimics the organic shapes of the plants beautifully, while also supplying plenty of nooks to play with while planting. We underplanted a tiny section at the front with purple pansies to add delicate texture and placed our foraged nest there as a springtime surprise. We've used river rocks as a substitute for eggs. Feel free to scatter pine needles (as we did) or other collected ephemera to finish off the vision.

PLANTS AND MATERIALS: *Hyacinthus orientalis* 'Woodstock' (hyacinth), *Matteuccia struthiopteris* (ostrich fern), *Viola* × *wittrockiana* (pansy), foraged nest, river rocks, pine needles

Pastel Prelude

Rather than trying to organize spring into a tidy planting, we've let the season's happy chaos reign here. The large, dark, bowl-shaped planter provides stability and grounding to let the pretty pastels shine. Plant in layers so that the shorter ones in front do not obscure the taller ones behind them. This enhances the visual depth and prevents overcrowding.

The double-flowered daffodil with white petals and peach centers serves as the focal point, providing a striking vertical element and subtle color that heralds spring. We've filled the center of our planter with these daffs, leaving room at the front and back for the rest of the plants.

The hellebore at the front and back of the planter adds a layer of lush greenery and blooms that start white then fade to pale green and contrast beautifully with the daffodils. Their evergreen foliage ensures interest even before the flowers bloom. With its deep red foliage, the heavenly bamboo acts as a natural accent off to one side of the planting. Finally, we placed freshly cut serviceberry branches to the back of the bowl, shooting straight up from the cluster of daffodils.

This planter's blooms will be over in early spring. Once the daffodils are finished, cut them back and add in late-spring and summer annuals (dahlias would be a wonderful addition come April—especially 'Sunshine' or 'Happy Single Kiss'). You can leave the daffodil bulbs for next year or remove and save them.

PLANTS AND MATERIALS:
Helleborus × *ericsmithii* 'Ivory Prince' (hellebore), *Nandina domestica* 'Jaytee' (aka Harbor Belle) (heavenly bamboo), *Narcissus* 'My Story' (daffodil), serviceberry branches

Natural Succession

Tulips are a perennial (pun intended) crowd-pleaser, blooming while winter still lingers and we're eager for any hint of spring. These deep 'Queen of Night' tulips, planted en masse, foreshadow the forthcoming summer spectacle of another perennial monoplanting, this time of the plume thistle. The two-season design of this planting is both fun and functional—make an effort once and enjoy two seasons of delightful displays.

Before adding soil and fertilizer, prepare the bowl of the planter with stones or pumice in the bottom third to support drainage (tulip bulbs are prone to rot; the pumice helps aerate the soil and keep soil moist, not soggy). If planting in fall, plant bulbs 6 inches (15 cm) deep and overwinter in a garage or insulated shed where they'll remain cool and protected from the elements. Bring the planter outside in spring, once the low temps are consistently at least 44°F (7°C). If planting in spring, look for forced tulips to add to the planter. Either way, plant the thistle throughout the planter in early spring, focusing on even distribution so you'll get a consistent field of color once they bloom. The nascent green of the spring thistle serves as a lush, leafy backdrop to the tulips' striking hue—but once summer hits, the plume thistle, with its vibrant pink blooms and remarkable height, will take center stage as the star of the show.

The stunning visual impact of this planter is reinforced by the pedestal and substantially sized bowl of the fiber cement pot, ideal for expansive plantings. The added height works especially well in a bed or along a path, so you never lose the visual interest among the in-ground plants.

PLANTS: *Cirsium rivulare* 'Atropurpureum' (plume thistle), *Tulipa* 'Queen of Night' (tulip)

Lines of Beauty

Though the beautiful branchwork of this living sculpture captivates year-round, it offers a special treat in spring when the rhododendron displays extraordinary, intensely scented blooms.

We love the 'Helen Everitt' rhododendron for its floral fragrance and wonderful white flowers, though fair warning—this delicate beauty usually loses a few buds during winter, so don't expect a full truss come spring. That said, this particular variety has a shallow root system and will survive happily in this type of planter.

The low bowl planter echoes the plant's own minimalist silhouette for perfect proportions that emphasize the overall serene feel. We've simply left this planter to naturalize with a wild moss understory; one can certainly help this along by foraging local mosses and relocating them to the planter.

PLANTS AND MATERIALS: *Rhododendron* 'Helen Everitt' (rhododendron), moss, river stone

Scents of Spring

Delicate and wild, with soft leaves and even softer colors, this sensational early-spring stunner is dripping in honeyed fragrance. It simply must be kept near the driveway, at the front porch, or beside the outdoor dining table so friends and family are greeted with its lovely perfume every time they step outside. The Korean spice viburnum is a shrub best known for its intoxicatingly fragrant white ball-shaped flowers and is an excellent choice for gardeners looking to add a woody element to their spring containers. Hyacinth, also known for its heady scent, is abundant—we decided to go for a light coral color to complement the subtle pink tones in the viburnum.

A tiered approach to planting, with the taller viburnum toward the back center of the pot and the shorter hyacinths and tulips around it, ensures that each plant can be appreciated without one overshadowing the others. The Solomon's seal emerges in graceful arches to unify the springtime bouquet. We added a mix of pine cones and pine needles to the base to further enhance the woodland feel.

If planted in a large pot (at least 18 to 24 inches/46 to 61 cm in diameter) with good drainage, and with consistent watering and spring fertilization, a viburnum can live a long time in a container. It can serve as a focal point year after year, with annuals changing in and out alongside it.

PLANTS AND MATERIALS: *Hyacinthus orientalis* 'Gipsy Queen' (hyacinth), *Polygonatum odoratum* 'Variegatum' (variegated Solomon's seal), *Tulipa* 'Candy Prince' (tulip), *Viburnum carlesii* (Korean spice viburnum), pine cones, pine needles

Wire Basket Bouquet

We rethought the fresh-cut bouquet for Mother's Day with this living, growing "bouquet." We kept the traditional spring color palette (a light blend of pinks, purples, and blues) and selected beloved seasonal varieties to anchor the design firmly in the holiday, but with planted varieties to make it a gift that lasts. Hellebore, our favorite harbinger of spring, adds structure, while frothy hydrangea and delicate pansies soften the overall feel. Our choice of buttercup offers a sweet citrus scent, and forget-me-nots nod to a sweet sentimentality.

These old German milk delivery crates are one of our quirkier potting shed staples—not only do they make cool planters, they're also practical (and pretty) repurposed as storage for tools, pots, and soils. Keep your eye out at auctions, estate sales, antique stores, and flea markets to start building your collection. To ensure the soil remains in place, we lined the crate with landscape fabric and tied it off with wire at the corners.

PLANTS: *Helleborus* 'Pippa's Purple' (Lenten rose), *Hydrangea macrophylla* 'Piihm-II' (aka Bloomstruck) (bigleaf hydrangea), *Myosotis scorpioides* (water forget-me-not), *Ranunculus asiaticus* 'Purple Picotee' (Persian buttercup), *Viola × wittrockiana* 'Plentifall Frost' (pansy)

A Classic Contrast

One of the joys of a container massing (see page 22) is that you can create an intentional ensemble focused on texture and color. Mixing boxwood and grasses, as we did here, allows for a visually appealing combination of structure and softness. It's also an opportunity to repurpose planters as the season progresses. These may all start out in a mass by the front door, but by the end of the season, maybe some have migrated to the outdoor dining table and others have made their way to the front porch.

To keep the grouping feeling intentional, we stuck with a green color palette for the plants and a neutral palette for the planters. These two visually cohesive elements allow us to experiment with a range of plant types, planter materials, and heights. The two boxwoods—'Wintergreen' and 'Green Velvet'—planted separately, have a similar spherical growth habit that helps create a nice rhythm through the grouping. The grasses also get their own containers, but placed close together create the illusion of a single planting, their wispy blades intermixing in the wind.

PLANTS: *Bouteloua gracilis* (blue grama grass), *Buxus* 'Green Velvet' (boxwood), *Buxus sinica* var. *insularis* 'Wintergreen' (Korean boxwood), *Carex* 'Everillo' (sedge), *Elymus magellanicus* (Magellan wheatgrass or blue wheatgrass)

Color Collective

In the same way we might choose furniture and décor based on the "bones" of our home's interior, we consider our home's exterior when we plant container gardens—especially if we're positioning our planters close to the building. Here we wanted a playful design to soften the stone facade without clashing with its natural beauty. The result is a charming vignette that feels inviting and fresh, ideal for a patio or entryway.

Using a tree in a planter is an effective way to add height and color to a spot that can't host a tree in the ground, like this concrete drive. We chose a tall Nikko maple for the largest of three planters. Its strong verticality and open branching, even when young, means it never obscures the nearby planters or architectural features that surround it. The smaller planters call back to this verticality in a petite form, with naturally topiary-shaped scented geraniums. The maple is underplanted primarily with cape primrose and lobelia, which are also used in the smaller planters to complete the look. The smaller planters also include aromatic herbs like rosemary, geranium, and creeping thyme, adding a sensory layer that's ideal if positioning this grouping by a doorway.

For the planters, we've chosen a cohesive color palette but varied the textures, shapes, and height. A low, wide bowl is a favorite for trees, as it gives the roots room to grow.

PLANTS: *Acer maximowiczianum* (Nikko maple), *Lobelia* 'Lobelix Lilac' (lobelia), *Streptocarpus* 'Lemon Sorbet' (cape primrose or lady slipper), *Thymus serpyllum* (creeping thyme), *Salvia rosmarinus* 'Prostratus' (creeping rosemary), *Pelargonium graveolens* 'Gray Lady Plymouth' (scented geranium)

Tulip Terrace

Tulips bloom early in the season, providing a welcome burst of color when few other plants are flowering. And when planted en masse? A truly stunning (and simple) spring display! As discussed on page 13, we're always putting our art school design principles to use when coming up with a container design. We like to work in odd numbers because the asymmetry keeps the eye engaged and moving through the composition, so here we've grouped five planters, each with a different tulip variety. The flowers' rainbow and the varying planter heights and shapes add visual interest and prevent monotony, while the tulips' complementary palette and the planters' uniform color and materiality create a cohesive, unified look. A single planter of paperwhites adds just enough contrast to the tulip-fest to give us that slightly imperfect look we love—nice to have, but not necessary.

If you intend to start your tulips from bulbs, you'll need to do so in fall. Bury them 6 inches (15 cm) deep and plant easy growers like kale and cabbages above them so you can enjoy the planter grouping through the colder months. Alternatively, head to your local nursery once spring arrives to find forced bulbs immediately ready for planting.

PLANTS: *Narcissus papyraceus* (paperwhites); *Tulipa* 'Blushing Impression', 'Horizon', 'Maria Kaczynska', 'Purissima', 'Siren Pink', and 'Toplips' (tulip)

Dappled Dogwood

When planting trees in containers, we'll often opt for a low, wide bowl to accentuate the specimen's striking silhouette and its magnificent size. Here a vintage-modern cement bowl serves as the perfect pedestal for the special variegated giant dogwood. Well-cultivated specimens display the distinct, layered branching that gives rise to its charming alternative moniker, the wedding cake tree. Indeed, from a distance, the frothy leaves almost appear purely white, but take a closer look and you'll find a green interior that's intricately serrated. Smaller or dwarf dogwood varieties are best for longer-term container use because their root systems are smaller. Dogwood will do better in the ground, but we successfully use small varieties in containers for two seasons before giving them a permanent home in the garden. That said, a dogwood could live for many years in a large planter. Either way, make sure you're watering frequently to help establish and grow the root system.

The sedge underplanting forms dense, arching clumps that sway gracefully with the wind, adding a soft, airy texture to the design. Licorice plant and trailing million bells mini petunia add even more color to the overall greenish-white palette, subtly echoing the tones of the variegated dogwood canopy.

PLANTS: *Calibrachoa* 'Uscal402-1' (aka Superbells Yellow Chiffon) (million bells), *Carex flacca* 'Blue Zinger' (blue-green sedge), *Cornus controversa* 'Variegata' (variegated giant dogwood or wedding cake tree), *Helichrysum petiolare* 'Lemon' (licorice plant)

Shade Seeker

This tall, compact planter is packed with deep color and a rich tapestry of textures. We've leaned heavily on perennials here, punctuating snowbush, astilbe, periwinkle, and delphinium with a few annuals like begonia and peperomia to ensure season-long color and interest. While you don't have to use this exact formula, we do recommend going for a wide breadth of varieties to achieve the grown-in look, as if these plants have naturally coexisted for some time. The perennials provide a fleetingly stunning display in early spring, creating a solid foundation so the later-arriving annuals can seamlessly take over as the perennials' blooms transform to lush foliage.

With their bold, graphic leaves, shredded umbrella plant and snowbush add an almost tropical element to the planting. This foliage-first approach is different from many classic spring designs, where we rightfully emphasize the flowers. That said, we do get some delicate color coming through with the beardtongue, periwinkle, delphinium, and gaura.

The dark fiberstone container offers a striking contrast to the vibrant greens, making the plants pop while enhancing the overall color scheme. Its textured surface adds another layer of intrigue, elevating the natural aesthetic of the arrangement.

PLANTS: *Ajuga reptans* 'Valfredda' (aka Chocolate Chip) (bugleweed), *Astilbe* 'Erica' (astilbe), *Begonia boliviensis* 'Bossa Nova Rose' (begonia), *Breynia disticha* 'Rosea Picta' (snowbush), *Delphinium grandiflorum* 'Summer Morning' (delphinium), *Oenothera lindheimeri* 'Walsilfou' (aka Walberton's Silver Fountain) (gaura), *Penstemon digitalis* (foxglove beardtongue), *Peperomia* 'Obtipan Citrus Twist' (peperomia), *Selaginella kraussiana* 'Gold Tips' (spikemoss), *Syneilesis aconitifolia* (shredded umbrella plant), *Vinca minor* 'Bowles Variety' (periwinkle)

Broad Strokes

Spring bursts forth in a kaleidoscope of colors, but there is an undeniable elegance to verdant greens. This arrangement is a study in the art of texture, weaving a monochromatic palette into a rich tapestry of tactile intrigue.

We planted the Japanese bird's nest fern at the back, so its bold, glossy leaves could establish a commanding presence. The feathery foliage of the blazing star introduces an ethereal element, and the artichoke thistle's serrated silvery leaves and thistle-like blooms add an edge to all the softness. Lamb's ear and the wormwood lend their signature fuzziness; the spurge contributes the most delicate white display.

We ground this arrangement with a weathered, rough-hewn barnacle planter. The earthy finish contrasts beautifully with the varying leaf textures, enhancing the composition's complexity. As the container grows in, each of the plant's inherent qualities will enhance the overall design. The upward-reaching ferns will continue to add height, contrasting sharply with the cascaders like the wormwood, creating a dynamic tension that will bring the design to life.

PLANTS: *Artemisia stelleriana* 'Silver Bullet' (beach wormwood or dusty miller), *Asplenium antiquum* (Japanese bird's nest fern), *Cynara cardunculus* 'Porto Spineless' (artichoke thistle), *Euphorbia* 'Diamond Mountain' (spurge), *Liatris spicata* 'Floristan White' (blazing star), *Stachys byzantina* 'Countess Helen von Stein' (lamb's ear), *Tinantia pringlei* (spotted widow's tears)

Hidden Gem

There's a spot at one of our stores that's lush with long grasses come mid- to late spring, which we keep untamed to maintain a natural buffer between the walkway and the buildings. We designed this container planting to both blend with the surrounding growth and make its own statement. From a distance, the bright color and textured foliage seem to float in the grass, capturing the imagination and drawing one closer to discover the planter itself.

This planter boasts many trailers and fillers for an ensemble show. Using a tiered planting approach to let all plants shine, we placed the tall vine maple at the center, mid-height plants like the flowering maple, astilbe, and coleus filling in the middle, and trailing plants like fuchsia and ivy cascading down the sides. The combination of fuchsias and coleus creates a soft, pinky red color palette that helps the planter stand out under the shade of the trees. Layering in silver and green tones (like those of the angel wings), tempers those warm tones, creating a balanced composition.

All the plants are well suited for shaded conditions, ensuring they thrive together in this low-light environment while bringing colorful interest to the shade understory in the trees.

PLANTS: *Abutilon* 'Marion' (flowering maple), *Acer circinatum* 'Ki setsudoe' (vine maple), *Astilbe chinensis* 'Vision in White' (Chinese astilbe), *Caladium* 'Candidum' (angel wings or heart of Jesus), *Fuchsia* 'Autumnale' (trailing fuchsia), *Fuchsia magellanica* 'Alba' (hardy fuchsia), *Fuchsia* 'Lord Beaconsfield' (fuchsia), *Hedera algeriensis* (Algerian ivy), *Begonia* Baby Wing series (begonia), *Polystichum munitum* (western sword fern), *Coleus scutellarioides* 'The Line' (coleus)

Confetti Sprinkle

Verbena serves as a colorful addition to spring gardens, where it is typically used in planters as a supporting character due to its trailing habit and vibrant hue. For this arrangement, we made it the star, choosing a complementary mix of purple, pink, and green varieties that evoke the joyful spirit of scattered blooms.

One of our favorite tricks for spring planters is to find hanging baskets that are dripping with grown-in, mature-size annuals and repurpose them into earthbound planters instead. These verbena were all in separate hanging baskets in the nursery, but we saw their potential—we popped them out of their plastic hanger pots and replanted them into this lovely textured faux bois planter. Made from cement to emulate a natural tree stump, this style of planter is at home in a number of settings, from woodland gardens to more structured landscapes. The trailing plants soften the edges of the planter and create a dynamic sense of movement, enhancing the naturalistic feel.

PLANTS: *Verbena* 'Veaz0013' (aka Lanai Lime Green), 'Veaz003' (aka Royal Peachy Keen), and 'Imagination' (verbena)

Made in the Shade

The ideal candidate for a sheltered spot on a front porch or patio awning, or in a shadowy garden corner, this spring planter is abundant with shade-loving specimens. We built our cache of plant varieties around the color of this antiquity-inspired planter—drawing out the rosy undertones with lots of pink-petaled flowers and blush-hued leaves. Because the color scheme is pretty pared back, we went wild with texture and shape, seldom repeating a single specimen, so that the overall composition can be appreciated anew from any angle.

Masterwort shoots up from the center of the planting; its delicateness contrasts effectively with the denser, ground cover foliage below. It boasts delicate variegated foliage and umbels of flowers reminiscent of angelica—a favorite among gardeners. The two varieties of *Lysimachia congestiflora* are enthusiastic growers, ensuring you'll have blooming color through spring. Additionally, houseplant varieties like the stromanthe, Australian fern, begonia, spurges, euphorbia, and ivy offer three-season interest (and can be replanted to live indoors).

As with many of our other many-specimen plantings, we placed the tallest plants in the center for verticality and planted the trailers around the perimeter so they can cascade gracefully over the sides. This design not only gives the planter a full, lush appearance but also ensures that each plant can be appreciated individually while contributing to the overall composition.

PLANTS: *Begonia boliviensis* 'Bossa Nova Pure White' (begonia), *Carex comans* 'Bronco' (leatherleaf sedge), *Euphorbia × martini* 'Km-mm024' (aka Miner's Merlot) (spurge), *Euphorbia hypericifolia* 'Balbreblus' (aka Breathless Blush) (euphorbia), *Euphorbia × martini* 'Ascot Rainbow' (spurge), *Hedera helix* 'Mini Esther' (English ivy), *Lysimachia congestiflora* 'Outback Sunset' (creeping jenny), *Lysimachia congestiflora* 'Persian Chocolate' (creeping jenny), *Nephrolepis obliterata* (Australian sword fern), *Peucedanum ostruthium* 'Daphnis' (masterwort), *Pilea microphylla* (artillery plant), *Salvia greggii* 'Lipstick' (autumn sage), *Stromanthe sanguinea* 'Triostar' (stromanthe), *Syngonium* 'Pink Splash' (arrowhead plant)

Spring's Shizen Balance

Shizen is a Japanese design principle that refers to a sort of spontaneous naturalness. However, its deeper meaning has evolved within Japanese culture and Zen Buddhist philosophy to encompass a broader concept of "human nature," uniting humanity and the natural world in harmony. Our interpretation here is a celebration of the ephemeral and lasting, short lived and enduring, combining the steady growth of a decades-old tree with the fleeting growth of spring flowers.

To wit, this Japanese andromeda tree has been growing in the same pot for fifteen years. The tree's mature branching and lush foliage serve as the central focal point, drawing the eye upward and providing a sense of grandeur and steady naturalness. Below it, spring's grape hyacinth and delicate toadflax add vibrant, cheerful color. Planted side by side and off-center, this group easily encompasses the idea of spring's spontaneous growth.

With its signature pastel color palette and abundance of enthusiastic bloomers, spring is the perfect season to reimagine an existing container with fresh underplantings. However, if you're starting with a fresh planter, plant the tree first, ensuring you pack enough soil to support the root ball. Leave about 1 to 2 inches (2.5 to 5 cm) of space at the top of the planter to prevent water from overflowing. Then underplant with your spring flowers, annual and perennial. The grape hyacinth is perennial in many zones and will come back next year to anchor the underplanting again.

PLANTS: *Linaria canadensis* (blue toadflax), *Linaria vulgaris* (yellow toadflax or butter-and-eggs), *Muscari* 'Big Smile' (grape hyacinth), *Pieris japonica* (Japanese andromeda or lily-of-the-valley shrub)

Chartreuse Charm

A sweet spring bloomer in the most gorgeous lime green, this petite hydrangea gets to show off its color when nestled atop a vibrant cushion of moss within a sleek, modern planter.

Cushion moss grows naturally in these neatly rounded clumps—little pillows of freshness. In the lushest complementary greens, the spongy moss and delicate hydrangea look cultivated, their rounded forms satisfyingly similar, almost like a piece of marshy land in a quiet corner of a botanical garden.

We chose a low, wide cement planter to give space for the moss to grow and to enhance the curving, soft lines of both the moss and the hydrangea. Versatile and charming, this arrangement works beautifully as a centerpiece, perched on a bench, or placed at the garden's edge as a focal point.

PLANTS: *Hydrangea macrophylla* 'Horwack' (aka Pistachio) (bigleaf hydrangea), *Leucobryum glaucum* (cushion moss)

Not-So-Traditional Topiary

We chose a white mandevilla as our topiary plant for its vining habit, continuous milky white blooms, and deep green foliage. While the green-and-white color palette may be a hallmark of a traditional topiary, the mandevilla's signature ethereal tendrils are anything but. As they begin to break free and grow in unexpected directions, the planting takes on a lived-in feeling, without the crisp lines or exacting trimming most topiaries have. Feel free to trim the vines as they grow if you'd like a more customary look, or let the tendrils run wild as the season progresses.

The mandevilla's untamed, wild spirit is mirrored in the relaxed, free-flowing understory below, featuring frothy euphorbia, delicate million bells, and two types of wormwood. The composition strikes a perfect balance—the topiary offers a strong, vertical anchor, while the cascading greenery below introduces softness and movement, creating a harmonious and captivating display. The planter echoes the plants' unconventional-yet-classic appeal: The footed silhouette is more traditional, while the aged texture gives a more casual feel.

PLANTS: *Artemesia stelleriana* 'Silver Bullet' (beach wormwood or dusty miller), *Artemisia schmidtiana* 'Silver Mound' (wormwood), *Calibrachoa* 'Cbrz0013' (aka Callie White) (million bells), *Euphorbia hypericifolia* 'Hip Hop' (euphorbia), *Euphorbia hypericifolia* 'Balbreblus' (aka Breathless Blush) (euphorbia), *Mandevilla* 'Madinia White' (mandevilla)

Garden Alcove

As the earth begins to reawaken and new life starts to sprout, we're happily surrounded by a diverse spectrum of greens, from soft blue-greens to vivid lime shades. We took advantage of this fleeting spring moment to create an informal, exuberant planting group.

Allowed to grow freely, spurge and wormwood tumble together with eucalyptus in a cluster of planters nestled under a weeping beech. The fine, almost feathery leaves of the wormwood contrast nicely with the rounder leaves of the spurge and eucalyptus, adding visual interest and a soft, ethereal quality. Typically, when grouping planters like this, we'll use an odd number of containers (three to seven, realistically). You want to ensure that the varying heights aren't competing with each other, but rather there's a sense of "nesting," like a lineup of Russian nesting dolls.

The little bowl in the front is a shallower container and gives opportunity to create a sculptural accent in the ensemble. We like using groupings of planters to highlight a corner or threshold; they can be easily peeled away to land on a bar or table when we're having company.

This casual arrangement creates a lively, unified display as the plants naturally intertwine, blending seamlessly and bringing a touch of brightness anywhere you need it. The relaxed, cascading growth blurs the boundaries between the individual plantings, resulting in an organic composition.

PLANTS: *Artemisia* 'Tnartms' (aka Makana Silver) (Maui wormwood), *Eucalyptus cinerea* (silver dollar eucalyptus), *Euphorbia × martini* 'Ascot Rainbow' (spurge)

Morning Mist

With subtle shifts in color, endless texture, and unruly height, this densely packed planter is a symphony of design. To achieve the serene dewy look, we've married cool white-green tones with purply blue pops of color. The mix of fine-textured foliage shooting upward with the broad leaves at the base offers a pleasing contrast that mimics the relaxed harmony of a well-tended English garden on a misty spring morning.

This is a dense planting, using a small number of a lot of plants to create visual impact. While you don't have to use all these plants to achieve the look, you'll want at least a few of each type: vertical grasses, tender blooms, delicate trailers, and short, broad-leaved plants. Here we started with the feather reed grass in the center, as it is the tallest. Feather reed grass is a low-maintenance fast grower that changes from reddish brown in spring to bleached gold in fall. Cypress vetch flowers from March until June and has nicely vertical leaves, so we added that next, right next to some pink masterwort and blue hyssop for even more color and height. Purply blue pops of tall verbena, sea holly, sage, hosta, and masterwort fill in at the front. We chose kidney weed, a popular lawn grass replacement, as the "ground cover" because its lush, clover-like leaves help keep the soil moist and brings the color all the way down.

PLANTS: *Agastache* 'Blue Boa' (hyssop or giant hyssop), *Ajuga reptans* 'Binblasca' (aka Black Scallop) (bugleweed), *Astrantia major* 'Westarpin' (aka Sparkling Stars Pink) (masterwort), *Calamagrostis × acutiflora* 'Karl Foerster' (feather reed grass), *Dichondra repens* (kidney weed), *Eryngium* 'Blue Jackpot' (sea holly), *Hosta* 'Blue Angel' (hosta), *Lathyrus ochrus* (Cyprus vetch), *Salvia guaranitica* 'Black and Blue' (anise sage), *Salvia nemorosa* 'May Night' (meadow sage), *Verbena bonariensis* (tall verbena or purpletop vervain)

Cascade in Coral

A modern silhouette and a pretty pastel palette combine in this bonsai-inspired design to create a perfectly balanced composition—an organic sculpture meant to be admired. Indeed, we've elevated this sunny bougainvillea in its simple rustic pot on a pedestal, so that it remains at eye level as one would showcase a piece of sculpture in an art museum. Pedestals are essential in our container planting tool kit for just this reason! We've pruned this bougainvillea specifically to mimic that artful bonsai-inspired silhouette, though its naturally sprawling growth pattern would still add a dynamic element to the composition.

This floriferous (profusely flowering) tropical thrives in hot weather; an ask that early spring's fickle weather can't surely deliver, especially as it is sensitive to frost. To give this planting its best chance, we recommend planting in late spring (after last frost, at least) so that it can come into its own once summer rolls around. Additionally, be sure to position this sun worshipper in a spot that gets at least six hours of direct sunlight. It requires regular watering, especially during dry spells. Ensure the soil is moist but not waterlogged.

PLANT: *Bougainvillea* × *buttiana* 'Afterglow' (bougainvillea)

Reaching New Heights

In this trellised planting, intertwining vines weave together like a botanical tapestry, wrapping around the vertical woven structure with a casual elegance that feels both spontaneous and considered. This planter will grow and change through the season—a sort of living art piece—as the different varieties reach their peak. The upright bugleweed and soft, ethereal blooms of the clematis add just the right pop of color, and even when the blooms fade, the interplay of foliage will keep things interesting, with delicate, wispy vines of the black-eyed Susan vine and passionflower creating lively contrast with broad, leathery leaves of the begonia and bright green of the chocolate mint.

The plants interact in a rhythmic way. Cascading elements spill over the edges of the container, adding a touch of controlled chaos, while the upward-reaching vines pull the eye skyward. It's all about creating movement and flow, making sure your gaze doesn't rest in one place for too long. It's as if the plants have simply found their way together over time—letting nature take the lead, with just a nudge in the right direction.

PLANTS: *Ajuga reptans* 'Bronze Beauty' (bugleweed), *Begonia rex-cultorum* 'Fedor' (rex begonia), *Clematis* 'Scented Clem' (aka Sugar-Sweet Blue) (clematis), *Dichondra argentea* (silver nickel vine), *Mentha × piperita* 'Chocolate' (chocolate mint), *Muehlenbeckia axillaris* (creeping wire vine or matted wire vine), *Passiflora incarnata* (purple passionflower or maypop), *Thunbergia* 'The Big White' (black-eyed Susan vine)

The Gathered Palette

By blending a variety of foliage with a few strategic pops of floral color, this display of diminutive planters makes a big impact. Ranging from 10 to 16 inches (25.5 to 40.5 cm) in diameter, the pots are small enough to group together on a front porch, in a garden bed, or on the back deck—just look for a well-trafficked spot that'll get the grouping its much-deserved attention.

For cohesion, we've kept the color scheme simple with an abundance of green, bright bursts of red, and a hint of yellow. We repeated some plant material across the various planters, leaning on English ivy as an easy-to-find filler, as well as nasturtium, geranium, and strawflower for their aesthetically interesting, verdant foliage. This continuity gives space for sculptural agave, colorful caladium, and mulla mulla to shine. As the ivy spreads out and the nasturtium blooms, the individual planters take on a collected, grown-in look. Planters in a mix of materials, sizes, and heights are key to getting dramatic visual impact, even at a small scale.

PLANTS: *Agave americana* 'Variegata' (variegated century plant), *Bracteantha bracteata* 'Klebb22100' (aka Mohave Fire Red) (strawflower), *Tropaeolum majus* 'Jewel of Africa' (nasturtium), *Pelargonium* 'Mrs. Pollock' (zonal geranium), *Ptilotus exaltatus* 'Regal Foxtail' (mulla mulla), *Hedera helix* 'Mini Esther' (English ivy), *Caladium* 'Pink Cloud' (angel wings or heart of Jesus), *Sambucus nigra* 'Eve' (aka Black Lace) (elderberry), *Plumbago auriculata* 'Monott' (aka Royal Cape) (cape plumbago)

SUMMER

As the days grow longer and the nights warmer, gardens hit their stride. The summer season is vibrant, lush, and unapologetically alive, with plants at their peak. It's time to push boundaries in your containers, celebrating the growing season's boldest colors, richest textures, and most dynamic plant pairings.

Summer is the season to reinvent your spring containers, swapping out early bloomers for heat-loving showstoppers that thrive in the sun. This time of year allows for dramatic, layered designs with cascading vines, tall grasses, and striking bright flowers—bold displays that capture the season's unstoppable energy. Summer is also perfect for experimenting with plants like tropicals, succulents, and fragrant herbs, which thrive in the sun and bring unique flair to outdoor spaces. It's a season that encourages outdoor living, and containers are a natural way to enhance patios, terraces, and entryways for gatherings and relaxation.

Summer Color Inspiration

Summer radiates energy and abundance, making it the ultimate season to experiment with fearless, vivacious color palettes in your garden and containers.

Verdant Silver

The lushness of green paired with the cool, elegant sheen of silver tones is a refreshing summer palette.

Eryngium giganteum 'Silver Ghost' (sea holly)

Artemisia ludoviciana 'Valerie Finnis' (western mugwort)

Begonia 'Silver Jewel' (begonia)

Cornus kousa 'Samzam' (aka Samaritan) (Korean dogwood)

Carex brunnea 'Variegata' (variegated sedge)

Echinacea purpurea 'White Swan' (coneflower)

Euphorbia hypericifolia 'Inneuphdia' (aka Diamond Frost) (euphorbia)

Petunia 'Revolution White' (aka Surfinia White) (petunia)

Daucus carota (Queen Anne's lace)

Sunset Blaze

The interplay of coral and pink makes reds appear richer and more luminous, creating a showstopping summer display of hot color.

Dahlia 'Bishop's Children' (dahlia)

Amaranthus tricolor 'Carnival' (summer poinsettia)

Coleus scutellarioides 'Uf12823' (aka Campfire) (coleus)

Hibiscus furcellatus 'Hawaiian Punch' (hibiscus)

Celosia argentea var. *cristata* 'Twisted Red' (celosia)

Zinnia elegans 'Benary's Giant Bright Pink' (zinnia)

Bougainvillea × *buttiana* 'Afterglow' (bougainvillea)

Echinacea SunSeeker series (coneflower)

Verbena 'Klevp15474' (aka Lascar Mango Orange) (verbena)

Cheerful Apricot

For an unexpected play on a tropical palette, move away from typical hot colors like bold yellow and red and instead elevate your design with a coral to gold color story.

Rosa **'Horcogjil'** (aka At Last) (rose)

Trifolium rubens **'Peachy Pink'** (clover)

Tropaeolum minus **'Just Peachy'** (nasturtium)

Verbena **'Peaches and Cream'** (verbena)

Linaria **'Peachy'** (toadflax)

Astilbe **'Rosa Perle'** (astilbe)

Nemesia **'Spicy Light Peach'** (nemesia)

Papaver pilosum **subsp.** *spicatum* (spiked poppy)

Oenothera lindheimeri **'Whirling Butterflies'** (gaura)

Buttery Blossoms

Bring the warmth of summer to life with soft, creamy yellows paired with delicate whites and fresh greens.

Celosia argentea var. *cristata* 'Bkcelflm' (aka Kelos Fire Lime) (celosia)

Dahlia 'Café au Lait' (dahlia)

Digitalis 'Dalmatian Crème' (foxglove)

Phygelius aequalis 'Yellow Trumpet' (cape figwort)

× *Petchoa* 'Sakpxc017' (aka SuperCal Light Yellow) (petchoa)

Persicaria virginiana 'Painter's Palette' (variegated knotweed)

Zinnia 'Isabellina' (zinnia)

Hylotelephium spectabile 'Elsie's Gold' (stonecrop)

Brunfelsia americana (lady of the night)

Floral Rambler

Pairing freewheeling plant life with a highly elegant urn creates a dialogue between the unbridled beauty of nature and the refined elegance of human design. A lush wild planting like this, full of fast-growing grasses, vines, and flowers, will transform quickly and dramatically as the season progresses. The stately urn, however, will not—providing a constant framework to highlight the natural changes within.

We chose to mix the jasmine, geranium, and impatiens because we knew their individual strengths would shine through (wispy texture, bold color, impressive height) while never working against their companions. The flowering elements here each contribute vibrant pops of the same shade of pink, allowing for their diverse leaf textures and distinct flower shapes to stand out without complicating the design. Plant the blue love grass and the reed grass in the center of the pot before adding any of the flowering varieties to help create that exuberant waterfall effect that cascades over the flowers.

Before planting the urn, line it with moss followed by landscape fabric; cut slits into the fabric to give roots and flowers access to the lower part of the urn. Once planted, be sure to water often and thoroughly; the fabric is porous and will dry out quickly.

PLANTS: *Cosmos bipinnatus* 'Candyfloss Red' (cosmos), *Dicranum scoparium* (mood moss), *Eragrostis elliottii* (blue love grass), *Impatiens × hybrida* 'Sakimp035' (aka SunPatiens Vigorous Shell Pink) (impatiens), *Jasminum officinale* 'Frojas' (aka Fiona Sunrise) (jasmine), *Pelargonium peltatum* 'Cascade Sofie' (ivy geranium)

Celestial Succulents

When the summer sun blazes and any reviving rain is scarce, succulents only get more radiant. This eclectic collection of echeveria, Bismarck palm, and cactus will remain effortlessly beautiful even in extreme conditions. We've focused our energy on scale and framing with this densely packed planter, trying to build overlapping "fields" of color and texture to dramatic effect.

The Bismarck palm is a graphic marvel, serving as the North Star, a striking centerpiece in the planting. Its unique washed-out blue hue echoes in the silver nickel vine that sits below it, spilling gracefully over the planter's edge. We've added a mix of echeveria varieties to introduce varying color and texture while maintaining some visual cohesion; feel free to experiment with the varieties your local nursery has in stock. Lavender scallops, cacti, and stonecrop finishes off the planting.

Folks often worry about combining succulents with other types of plants, thinking they have opposing water and sun needs. But the truth is, succulents are happily at home alongside other seasonal plants, provided they're not in damp, shady spots. Mixing like-minded plants that don't seem to "go" at first glance often yields the most dynamic and visually appealing combinations.

The cool tones—all silvers, greens, and purples—create a cohesive, calming palette that feels modern and fresh juxtaposed against the stunning black terra-cotta urn.

PLANTS: *Aeonium* 'Blushing Beauty' (aeonium), *Bismarckia nobilis* (Bismarck palm), *Dichondra argentea* 'Silver Falls' (silver nickel vine), *Echeveria* 'Stella Blanc' (echeveria), *Echeveria* 'Red Velvet' (echeveria), *Echeveria runyonii* 'Topsy Turvy' (echeveria), *Echeveria lilacina* (ghost echeveria), *Graptopetalum paraguayense* subsp. *bernalense* (Bernal ghost plant), *Hylotelephium telephioides* (Allegheny stonecrop), *Kalanchoe fedtschenkoi* (lavender scallops), *Rhipsalis baccifera* (mistletoe cactus), *Sempervivum* 'Blue Whale' (hens and chicks), *Sedum spurium* 'Tricolor' (stonecrop)

Far Afield

This "more is more" planter is a vibrant, sun-soaked ode to high summer, showcasing how a mix of diverse plants can create lush harmony. The lemony yellow and bright green color palette feels just right for the season, and the abundance of plant types celebrates summer's natural riches.

When we're filling containers like this, we find we often need more plants than originally planned. For maximum impact, this 36-inch-wide, 30-inch-tall (91 cm wide, 76 cm tall) container packs in greenery. A good rule is two to three plants per 12 inches (30.5 cm) of diameter, which means eighteen to twenty-seven plants for a container of this size. In this design, eleven different varieties—including trailing sweet potato vine, coleus, and verbena—are packed tightly together so the plants feel stacked on top of one another. We planted the purple fountain grass in the middle but off to the side, like a firework exploding from the center. The Cake Pops Pink verbena has just a hint of pink, playing off the fountain grass color. The two types of euphorbia add a fine, mist-like texture to the outer edges.

To finish it off, the rustic, weathered planter adds character and timeless appeal, while its robust, bulbous shape supports the volume and anchors the arrangement in its garden setting.

PLANTS: *Chamaecyparis obtusa* 'Nana Lutea' (dwarf golden hinoki cypress), *Coleus scutellarioides* 'Kakegawa Ce2' (aka ColorBlaze Chocolate Drop) (coleus), *Euphorbia × martini* 'Ascot Rainbow' (spurge), *Euphorbia hypericifolia* 'Inneuphdia' (aka Diamond Frost) (euphorbia), *Heuchera* 'Obsidian' (coralbells), *Ipomoea batatas* 'Tricolor' (sweet potato vine), *Juniperus virginiana* 'Grey Owl' (eastern red cedar), *Lantana montevidensis* (weeping lantana), *Pennisetum setaceum* 'Rubrum' (purple fountain grass), *Coleus scutellarioides* 'Balcenna' (aka Henna) (coleus), *Plectranthus argentatus* (silver spurflower)

Copper Tone

Because summer blesses us with an abundance of gorgeously colored, richly textured botanicals every year, our inclination is often to mix as many plants as we can into a single container. Sometimes, though, it's fun to let a couple varieties speak for themselves (and to each other).

The bold structure of the aloe offers a striking contrast to the soft frills of the hummingbird mint and feathery sedge. Color plays an important role here, too—the copper patina of the planter picking up the blue undertones of the aloe and the pink-oranges of the hummingbird mint and sedge, creating a sunset-over-the-water effect. This blend of blues, peaches, and brown is a rare but sophisticated color combination.

When planting the aloe, opt for one slightly off-center placement toward the back edge of the planter and another more forward and central. This allows the sedge and hummingbird mint to fill in on all sides of the statement plants, for that natural, grown-in look we love. The broad, open shape of this planter allows ample space for the plants to spread out as summer wears on. And yes, the hummingbird mint is both fragrant and attracts the fast-flapping creatures, a sweet bonus.

PLANTS: *Aloe wickensii* (geelaalwyn), *Agastache aurantiaca* 'Apricot Sprite' (hummingbird mint), *Carex buchananii* 'Red Rooster' (sedge)

Tangerine Dream

Moving away from a more restrained (and obvious) summer rose container, this design puts an elegant tea rose on riotous display, playing up the wild, English garden elements a rose planting can take on.

The 'At Last' rose, with its soft coral blooms and plentiful petals, is the star of this planter, offering a splash of color that stands out against a lush green backdrop. We're particularly fond of this cultivar because it performs all summer long and boasts a heady, floral fragrance. The sedge adds wispy texture, its airiness balancing out the robustness of the roses. The rust brown sedge acts as a foil to the apricot color of the rose, while the hummingbird mint reinforces the peachy tones. Smaller, trailing plants at the base of the container add depth and fill out the arrangement.

The solid, earthy appearance of this rustic planter forms a striking contrast with the delicate beauty of the roses. The container's substantial size allows for adequate root growth, essential for the health of the roses, and its classic shape complements the timeless appeal of the flowers.

PLANTS: *Agastache* 'Kudos Gold' (hummingbird mint), *Begonia semperflorens* 'Linda Dawn' (white wax begonia), *Carex buchananii* 'Red Rooster' (sedge), *Euphorbia hypericifolia* 'Inneuphdia' (aka Diamond Frost) (euphorbia), *Rosa* 'Horcogjil' (aka At Last) (rose)

Peas, Please

A crowd-pleaser that's equal parts effortless beauty and culinary trendsetter, butterfly pea is an easy-growing climber that's revered for its edible blue flowers. Use the petals to dye fabric or as a natural food coloring, or brew the petals for a delicious tea—add lemon juice to watch the color magically morph into a bright purple.

As a native to regions in southern Asia and India, *Clitoria ternatea* is a sun worshipper, making it ideal for summer gardens (though it's happy to overwinter in a sunny window). The twining, outward-growing vines can grow up to 10 feet (3 m), but our choice of a more diminutive trellis height and planter diameter should keep the growth to a tidy 3 feet (1 m) overall. That said, be sure to choose a trellis that is about 3 inches (7.5 cm) smaller in diameter than the planter itself yet can expand vertically to grow with the plant. As the butterfly pea starts to grow and expand outward, you can delicately loop the vines through the trellis openings to persuade the growth upward.

PLANT: *Clitoria ternatea* (butterfly pea)

Bloom Boom

Some planters you dream up to excite, inspire, and satisfy your own green fantasies, and others you plant to salute someone else—as we did here, in a design celebrating a dear friend's favorite color combination, vivid red and cool lavender. A living tribute to friendship, fun, and the joy of gardening, it is meant to capture the interconnectedness of enduring memory and natural beauty.

Planted in late spring, this container promises a spectacular summer show. Russian sage, dahlias, and mandevilla dominate with their long, leggy blooms, ensuring a continuous burst of color. The blue-hued Russian sage in the center provides a cool, calming counterpoint to the fiery reds, while begonias spill gracefully over the edge of the planter; as they grow, out and down, there's potential for them to take root in crevices for an unexpected touch of wild beauty. Mandevilla is typically planted with a trellis; here we've done without it, allowing the plant to explore its free-spirited habit, stretching upward and trailing downward and adding to the dynamic flow of the arrangement.

PLANTS: *Achillea millefolium* (yarrow), *Dahlia* 'Catching Fire' (dahlia), *Salvia yangii* (syn. *Perovskia atriplicifolia*) (Russian sage), *Mandevilla splendens* (red mandevilla), *Salvia farinacea* (mealy sage), *Saxifraga stolonifera* 'Tricolor' (variegated strawberry begonia)

Desert Meadow Harmony

Felicia amelloides 'Variegata', commonly known as the variegated blue daisy, is a charming and decorative plant that stands out due to its attractive foliage and dainty blue flowers, which add a vibrant splash of color to gardens and attract pollinators. The most striking feature of variegated blue daisy is its leaves; the cream or white edges contrast beautifully against a green center and serve as a perfect foil to the flower. It typically forms a low-growing, compact mound, making it ideal as a trailer to fall across the edge of a planter.

To break up the cloud mass of daisies, we added some sculptural aloe to our planter. A desert-inspired harmony exists between the delicate daisies with their soft, ruffled foliage unruly against the structured architecture of the aloe leaves. The bluebeard and blue dwarf ruellia both add a vivid purple hue. The end result is a planting perfect for high summer when the four varieties can thrive in the warmer temperatures, and their similar coloring gives this composition a subtle, mono-planting look. The textural ceramic planter brings an earthly naturalism to the overall design, keeping it from becoming too one-note or modern.

PLANTS: *Aloe vera* (aloe), *Felicia amelloides* 'Variegata' (variegated blue daisy), *Caryopteris × clandonensis* 'Blue Mist' (bluebeard), *Ruellia simplex* 'Katie' (dwarf ruellia)

Sculpture Garden

A successful planting always needs a focal point—something that draws the eye and anchors the look. While the instinct is to let the plants take center stage, the right planter can become a statement piece of its own, elevating the design. These containers are exactly that—dynamic and cool. Greg snagged them at an auction, and they're heavy, made from angular, modern Corten steel. They're more than just containers; these art pieces outshine the plants they hold, which is exactly the point.

To emphasize the sculptural form and striking materiality of these planters, we opted for a monochromatic palette and a clean, minimalist arrangement. We chose tidy, upright plants like the 'Silver Gumdrop' coralbells and the bugleweed and sage for their bold foliage and vertical blooms. Their clean silhouettes harmonize with the planters' architectural lines, delivering a graphic, modern aesthetic perfectly suited for summertime shade.

Positioned on a staircase, the planter duo creates a bold statement, drawing the eye and elevating the plants' vibrant colors above the surrounding greenery. The cool purple tones of the plants provide a striking contrast to the lush greens and whites of the surrounding garden, while the rusted finish of the Corten planters introduces a complementary orange hue for added depth of color.

PLANTS: *Ajuga reptans* (bugleweed), *Heuchera* 'Silver Gumdrop' (coralbells), *Sedum* (stonecrop), *Salvia* 'Midnight Model' (sage), *Schizachyrium scoparium* 'Chameleon' (little bluestem)

Sunbeam

The popcorn plant (*Senna didymobotrya*) is a showstopping addition to any container design, captivating with its bright green, pinnate leaves that release an uncanny buttered popcorn scent—a delightful novelty sure to spark conversation! While the aroma adds a playful charm, it's crucial to note that this plant is toxic if ingested, so choose its location with care.

Native to Central and Eastern Africa and hardy in USDA Zones 9 and 10, the popcorn plant thrives as an annual in cooler climates. Its towering form, vibrant yellow blooms, and tropical aesthetic bring height and drama to summer gardens. Requiring full sun, it's a favorite of pollinators, further enhancing its garden appeal.

For a complementary underplanting, we paired it with 'Moonbeam' tickseed, petunia, and coneflower to evoke a festive confetti effect with the textured leaves. The addition of orange New Zealand sedge, with its fiery orange-yellow tips glowing in the afternoon sun, ties the limited color palette together. And rather than minimize the whimsy with a more traditional planter shape, we decided to play up the lighthearted design with a fluted and stretched-out UFO-inspired planter.

PLANTS: *Carex testacea* 'Prairie Fire' (orange New Zealand sedge), *Coreopsis verticillata* 'Moonbeam' (tickseed), *Echinacea* 'Cheyenne Spirit' (coneflower), *Petunia* 'Cascadias Indian Summer' (petunia), *Senna didymobotrya* (popcorn plant)

All Fired Up

The lusciousness of summer blooms is still on riotous display in this late-season planter pairing. Exuberant and joyful, this super-saturated planting encourages experimentation and play—adding a second planter on a riser instantly boosts the overall theatricality of the final product. The showy tonal palette of neon magenta, deep red, and washed pink keeps it cohesive and mimics a garden's natural color saturation after an afternoon thunderstorm.

Position your planters and riser before planting; we suggest a driveway edge or similarly breezy spot to maximize easy in-the-round viewing. Starting at the back perimeter of the elevated planter, place fast-growing, tall varieties like summer poinsettia, celosia, and sage. Continue to work back to front, adding zinnias, summer poinsettia, and hibiscus in the center. Plant trailers like bougainvillea and vinca around the edges. For the lower planter, focus on compact, mounding varieties like sage and coneflower that stay controlled in height, allowing the elevated planter to maintain its dramatic impact without interference.

The key here is to pack a lot of plants into the soil—don't be afraid to exploit every inch of dirt available. These planters are meant to be transitory as the season progresses, so happy cohabitation between blooms doesn't have to be a major consideration. You can always replace spent flowers with fresh ones to keep telling your color story through the season.

PLANTS: *Amaranthus tricolor* 'Carnival' (summer poinsettia), *Bougainvillea × buttiana* 'Rosenka' (bougainvillea), *Catharanthus* 'Quasar Salmon Target' (vinca), *Celosia argentea* var. *cristata* 'Twisted Red' (celosia), *Echinacea purpurea* 'Rainb299' (aka Rainbow Marcella) (coneflower), *Hibiscus furcellatus* 'Hawaiian Punch' (hibiscus), *Salvia* 'Wendy's Wish' (sage), *Coleus scutellarioides* 'Uf12823' (aka Campfire) (coleus), *Zinnia elegans* 'Benary's Giant Bright Pink' (zinnia)

A Ghostly Begonia

Houseplants are often happiest outside during the summer months—a literal breath of fresh air for our favorite indoor greens. If you have the room, haul your houseplants outside once the threat of frost is gone and watch them thrive. Just be sure they're getting enough water; the direct heat can leave them thirsty far quicker than when they're indoors.

This "ghost" begonia, with its dark purple stems and spectral gray-green leaves, plays well with the muted blue planter—and it looks especially glowy nestled under the cover of your favorite sitting tree (beloved for its indoor hardiness, this begonia will do just as well in a shady area of the garden). The delicate, wispy variegated sedge adds movement and softness, which contrasts nicely against the more robust, veined leaves of the begonia.

PLANTS: *Begonia rex-cultorum* 'Harmony's Ghost Whisperer' (rex begonia), *Carex oshimensis* 'Fiwhite' (aka EverColor Everest) (Japanese sedge)

The Old Romantic

This planter feels plucked out of time, with an abundance of blossoms and a lush underplanting of jewellike succulents. Mixing formal and informal elements in garden design creates a dynamic, visually engaging planting that feels both refined and organic. Our formula: Start with a classic urn, geometric planter, or traditional container. Add structure with a gardenia, boxwood, or evergreen, then underplant with cascading foliage, varied textures, and a mix of heights to introduce controlled chaos and soften the composition.

Here we went geometric with a robust Corten steel vessel with rivets and angles, which brings industrial charm and antique appeal. Its substantial size and ornate design anchor the arrangement, providing a striking contrast to the organic forms of the plants. A topiary gardenia, prized for its glossy green leaves and fragrant white blooms, serves as the focal point, adding both beauty and a sensory experience to the design. The gardenia is surrounded by succulents and sedums, including rosette-forming varieties and trailing plants that spill over the edges, so that the eye has many different spots to rest. The disparate elements create a captivating visual tension, blending architectural structure with botanical complexity.

PLANTS: *Dichondra argentea* 'Silver Falls' (dichondra), *Echeveria* 'Blue Curls' (echeveria), *Gardenia jasminoides* 'Fortuniana' (gardenia or cape jasmine), × *Graptoveria* 'A Grim One' (graptoveria), mixed sedum mat/roof tile, *Curio serpens* (blue chalk sticks)

Blue Skies

This entire arrangement is designed around an architectural locust branch—one of our favorite ways to begin a planting. There's nothing better than finding a "good branch" on a nature walk; perfectly gnarled and twisted, foraged branches can add so much dynamism to a planter.

We spray-painted this one silver to complement the zinc planter's metallic tones; this step is definitely not required, but we thought it made the branch feel more intentional and played up its natural twisty shape.

While the branch is the focal point, we actually added it last. Instead, we started with the plumbago and rosemary, mixing both together to fill in most of the planter. They cascade gracefully over the edges, softening the design and blending into the lush surroundings. The rosemary adds a fresh herbal scent, while its delicate texture balances the plumbago's bold blue-green foliage. It took a few tries for us to find the right spot for the branch; we simply inserted it into the soil and stepped back from the planter each time to assess the overall look. We finally landed with the branch centered nearer to the front, its thicker end buried firmly in the soil.

PLANTS AND MATERIALS: *Plumbago auriculata* 'Imperial Blue' (cape plumbago), *Salvia rosmarinus* (rosemary), zinc-painted locust branch (any branch with character will do)

Willow Work

Willow whips are the cut branches of willow trees—those long, flexible branches that nod earthward and are often used as garden structures, woven together for structural integrity and visual interest. They are valued for their incredible flexibility and strength and can be bent and twisted without breaking, making them ideal for weaving intricate patterns and designs. Willow weaving is a crafting method that dates back to the Bronze Age, and has been used across many cultures since, in basketry, garden architecture, and even in the construction of living willow sculptures and fences. We've always wanted try the idea, and since these branches are easily rooted in containers, we thought, *Why not give it a go?*

To begin, you must harvest and prepare the willow. Willow whips are best cut in late winter to early spring, when the sap is down and the branches are most flexible. Before weaving, soak the whips in water for three to seven days (depending on their thickness and dryness), until they are supple and pliable. This step is essential to prevent cracking or breakage during bending.

Next, prepare the container. Thoroughly soak the soil in your container before inserting the whips—this softens the medium and helps anchor the willow securely. Mark out a circle (we used an 12-inch/30.5 cm diameter) and insert the willow whips evenly spaced around the perimeter. Push each one 3 or 4 inches (8 to 10 cm) into the soil for stability.

Now it's time to weave the willow. Choose a starting whip and bend it across the one directly next to it, weaving in an alternating pattern: over the next, under the following, and so on around the circle. As you complete one round, begin weaving higher, keeping the same over-under rhythm. Each successive layer spirals slightly upward, creating a basket-like form. Secure the whips as you go: Use flexible bonsai wire to secure intersections where needed—every 6 inches (15 cm) is a good guide. This helps maintain the shape as the structure grows in height. Step back periodically and adjust the whips for even tension and loose symmetry. Once your structure reaches the desired height, trim the tops for a tidy finish or allow them to flare outward for a wilder effect.

We went for a single-specimen underplanting (of tickseed) to keep the focus on the willow. A dark gray fiber cement planter anchors the otherwise delicate planting. The teak feet are an important lift for proper drainage that also add a natural element to the bottom of the overall composition that echoes the willow whips. Willow likes a lot of water, so be sure to water often to keep the soil from drying out.

PLANTS: *Coreopsis verticillata* 'Zagreb' (tickseed), *Salix viminalis* (basket willow or common osier)

Garden Art

Incorporating cacti and other structural plants into a container arrangement is a fantastic strategy for creating a standout display in the garden. Here we've paired simple, unassuming planters with the whimsical and strange string of bananas and euphorbia—their dramatic height (or lack thereof) with unusual branching is so fun and playful.

With its spectral hue and sculptural silhouette, the 'White Ghost' euphorbia is an especially sought-after specimen by collectors, making it a fun Easter egg for fellow enthusiasts who may happen upon the container grouping. Its grayish-blue color is striking, as are its papery "arms," which contribute to its ghostly appearance. The string of bananas is a popular houseplant choice for its Seussian physicality, all droopy trails and tiny, banana-shaped leaves.

In our Zone 6b gardens, we overwinter succulents so our spring, summer, and early autumn containers can be filled with these architectural gems. There are so many shades, shapes, and textures to pair together, and they're low maintenance, too, needing only sporadic watering, so you can enjoy your summer vacation. Both varieties shown here are easy to propagate as well. Simply cut a healthy, mature stem just below the node and allow it to dry out for a few days in the potting shed or kitchen counter. Prepare soil as you would for a fresh planter, insert the propagated piece cut side down, and water thoroughly.

PLANTS: *Curio radicans* (string of bananas), *Euphorbia lactea* 'White Ghost' (euphorbia)

Fiery Plumes

'Pink Champagne' ruby grass is a clumping annual with beautiful amethyst-pink flowers that open up into fluffy plumes. It carries well into fall, with the grass turning bluish green and the flowers' blooms fading to a silvery white. This long-lasting visual interest, paired with the plant's ability to grow fast and withstand heat, makes it a popular choice to line garden beds and act as filler to more complicated container designs.

We've done neither of those things here, though, and instead singled out the grass to fully appreciate its seasonal beauty. It's the stately urn planter that elevates this otherwise super-pared-back planter. The pot's classic shape adds a touch of traditional charm to the design, while its robust size makes it a focal point without overshadowing the delicate textures of the grass itself.

PLANT: *Melinus nerviglumis* 'Pink Champagne' (ruby grass)

Sun-Worn Days

We love the stretch of end-of-summer planters; this one takes center stage in the late-summer garden. This transitional design features a wonderfully grown-in agave plant, fragrant rosemary at its peak, some stretched succulents, and a simple pea gravel topper, all packed into an antiquity-inspired urn.

We'd already planted the rosemary in this urn at the start of the season, and we gathered the agave and succulents from other summer planters. That said, you can start fresh with the late-summer options at your local nursery. (Bonus points: These are the varieties often on end-of-season sale!)

Either way, you'll want to plant the rosemary first and *almost* fill the planter with it, leaving just enough room for the agave. We've positioned our agave off-center so it leans to one side, stretching to meet the autumn sun. The summer-grown succulents trail over the sides of the planter and introduce varied texture and subtle color differences, the brownish pink hearkening back to the traditional fall palette. We've positioned our planter near a grassy border to play up its wild-grown feel, but it would also look at home on a driveway or at the entry.

PLANTS AND MATERIALS: *Agave attenuata* 'Agavws' (aka Ray of Light) (variegated fox tail agave), *Salvia rosmarinus* (rosemary), × *Graptosedum* 'California Sunset' (graptosedum), × *Pachyveria* 'Simonoasa' (variegated echeveria), *Aloe rebmannii* (aloe), pea gravel

Purple Moon

Hanging baskets brimming with petunias, begonias, and geraniums are a quintessential feature of summer porches and pergolas. Inspired to rethink this tradition, we flipped it—literally. Using a spindle-shaped planter that mimics the silhouette of a hanging basket, we directly transplanted nursery-grown hanging baskets for a fresh, bold look.

Indeed, it's the planter we're hoping to highlight with this design. The spindle fiber cement planter by Willy Guhl, otherwise known as the Diablo planter, is an iconic example of Guhl's quintessential low-effort, maximum statement philosophy, with its hourglass silhouette and rough-hewn texture. Guhl was a nineteenth-century Swiss architect and a pioneer in the "neo-industrial" movement, championing furniture and garden designs that were both incredibly simple and high functioning. He's well known for his innovative use of fiber cement as a material in chairs and planters specifically. Fiber cement is well loved for its solid, all-weather materiality that ages beautifully.

To ensure the interesting textures of the plants really stand out, we've stuck close to an all-green color palette, varying the hues slightly. The string of bananas tumbles downward en masse, the mangave is a spiky standout, and the creeping blue sedum's compact, layered leafing fills in the gaps. Our two verbena varieties add a most welcome pop of purple, which is echoed in the leaves of the mangave. The asymmetrical planting helps break up the natural symmetry of the spindle planter.

PLANTS: × *Mangave* 'Moon Glow' (mangave), *Sedum hispanicum* (creeping blue sedum), *Curio radicans* 'Glauca' (string of bananas), *Verbena canadensis* 'Homestead Purple' (verbena), *Verbena rigida* (Cake Pops Purple) (tuberous verbena)

Orchid Odyssey

Container plantings are fantasy worlds—worlds where the ephemeral, the strange, and the quixotic come together to create magic. We embraced this spirit with this particular design, planting orchids and succulents together in the same container because it's artful and fun, not because it's practical or long-lasting (it's neither!). In fact, we knew we were going to raise a few eyebrows. But that's the beauty of container planting; it's about creating a moment, a conversation, a story—and what a wonderfully unique story this is.

Orchids love humidity and shy away from direct light. Succulents thrive in arid conditions and are sun worshippers. Below the surface, however, both prefer well-draining soil and hate sitting in water, which means this unlikely pairing can thrive in the same pot for at least a little while. By planting the two different plant types in distinct zones within the container, you'll gain a little more control over watering and sun exposure.

Using the natural teak planter and a combination of additional ornamental elements like moss, kiwi vine, and stone toppers, we've created a dimensional landscape that feels like a little slice of the rainforest landed on your tabletop. This planter is about 24 inches (61 cm) long and 16 inches (40.5 cm) wide, making it the perfect size for a dinner party centerpiece. Once your event is over, move the container to a spot that receives daily filtered light, like on a covered patio or under a pergola, and enjoy it. These plants will fare well together for a few weeks; after that, replace plants that look unhealthy to freshen the container for the next time it will be used as a centerpiece!

PLANTS: *Ludisia discolor* (jewel orchid), *Oncidium varicosum* var. *rogersii* 'Baldin' (Rogers' dancing lady orchid), *Phalaenopsis* 'Fangmei Green Light' (moth orchid), *Paphiopedilum* Wössner Helene Green Charlene group (lady's slipper orchid), *Sempervivum* 'Pacific Blue Ice' (hens and chicks), *Sempervivum* 'Pink Charm' (hens and chicks), *Sempervivum* 'Casa' (hens and chicks)

Firetail Meadow

Persicaria is a genus of flowering plants in the buckwheat family (Polygonaceae). New *Persicaria* hybrids are brighter and more controlled than their natural counterparts—and just as gorgeous, capturing the hearts of gardeners who cherish the untamed essence of perennials and aspire to re-create the wild beauty of meadows within their curated landscapes.

Here the mountain fleece duo works together as a singular, showstopping entity that looks especially stunning in summer's raking light. Its wispy stems dance in the wind, while the lush green switchgrass below give depth and texture to the design, a bucolic celebration of the wildflower meadow. To bolster the unified feeling, we've mixed the two *Persicaria* varieties together in the planting; they'll look even more connected as they mature.

Since this design's playful personality comes from only three plants, the visual impact results from planting en masse—we want it to look like we dug up a piece of the prairie and plopped it into a container. A spacious, estate-size planter is essential to achieve this grown-in look, as is planting the grasses around the edges of and in between the mountain fleece varieties, giving room for the lively bloomers to show off their color and height.

PLANTS: *Panicum virgatum* 'Niagara Falls' (switchgrass), *Persicaria amplexicaulis* 'Firetail' (mountain fleece or knotweed), *Persicaria amplexicaulis* 'Fat Domino' (mountain fleece or knotweed)

Bountiful Beauty

Summer is the season of childhood nostalgia—all cloud watching, firefly chasing, and making flower crowns in the meadow—and this Mexican daisy planting perfectly captures that wild freedom of youth.

Delicate yet robust, *Erigeron karvinskianus* is a charming, resilient daisy with fine foliage and delicate petals that start white and slowly mature to a soft pink as summer rolls on. When planted in the garden, it spreads quickly, forming a low, mounting ground cover, and will also happily flourish in whatever container you put it in, cascading and expanding with an understated elegance that sighs with summer nonchalance. It blooms from early spring through autumn, offering a long-lasting display that attracts bees and butterflies. To reinforce the casual note of this airy, wild feeling, we've planted the daises unevenly, with a huge cloud taking up a third of the planter, leaving the remaining two-thirds sparse. The low bowl keeps the entire thing (literally) grounded and at a child's natural eye level for an extra hint of whimsy.

PLANT: *Erigeron karvinskianus* (Mexican daisy)

AUTUMN

As temperatures begin to dip and evenings lengthen, we return to the familiar rhythms of harvest season—a time to reinvigorate your outdoor spaces to fully embrace the cozy, communal spirit of autumn. Blend the bounty of the harvest with the artistry of design by embracing rich, warm color palettes, textured foliage, and hardy blooms that thrive in cooler temperatures.

A season of abundance and change, fall offers an opportunity to embrace the unique beauty of nature's shift from vibrant growth to quiet dormancy. Now is the time to hold a mirror up to the garden: Reflect on the ornamental grasses, high-summer perennials, and colorful-foliage plants that have taken on new form in the transition from summer to fall; celebrate them; and tidy it all up again, adding some fresh color and removing some spent plants.

Fall is also a time to plan for the future, with containers featuring plants that transition seamlessly into winter, such as evergreen shrubs or decorative conifers. These designs not only honor the season but also extend their beauty and impact as the year progresses. Planting in fall is about embracing change and celebrating the fleeting yet memorable characteristics of the season.

Autumn Color Inspiration

Autumn is a season of warmth and transformation, where the landscape shifts to a symphony of rich, earthy tones and soft, golden light.

Sapphire Shadow

Dramatic black and blue plants bring a moody ambience to autumn planters, with silvery or blue foliage or soft ornamental grasses for contrast and texture.

***Dahlia* 'Black Monarch'** (dahlia)

***Ocimum* 'African Blue'** (African blue basil)

***Amaranthus hypochondriacus* 'Lotus Purple'** (amaranth)

***Hylotelephium telephium* 'Black Jack'** (stonecrop)

***Ophiopogon planiscapus* 'Nigrescens'** (black mondo grass)

***Dahlia* 'Karma Choc'** (dahlia)

Schizachyrium scoparium (little bluestem)

***Capsicum annuum* 'Black Pearl'** (ornamental pepper)

Cosmos atrosanguineus (chocolate cosmos)

Rosewood Autumn

A palette of pinks, from soft blush to vibrant coral, balanced by rich browns pairs beautifully with copper-toned grasses and foliage, and is a perfect foil to heirloom pumpkins.

Celosia argentea var. *plumosa* 'Rainbow Sherbet Mix' (celosia)

Pennisetum orientale 'Karley Rose' (fountain grass)

Echinacea 'Fresco Apricot' (coneflower)

Dahlia 'Gallery Leonardo' (dahlia)

'Fairytale', 'Autumn Buckskin', and 'Black Futsu' pumpkins

Hylotelephium erythrostictum 'Frosty Morn' (stonecrop)

Zinnia elegans 'Queen Red Lime' (zinnia)

Hydrangea paniculata 'Limelight' (panicle hydrangea)

Aster pyrenaeus 'Lutetia' (Pyrenean aster)

Garden Bounty

Our harvest planter is rooted in the celebration of nature's generosity during the autumn season. This design draws upon the vivid colors, varied textures, and plentiful yields associated with this time of year, creating a tableau that is both visually stunning and emotionally evocative.

Over summer, we added the Virginia creeper to the planter so it would be filled in and trailing by fall. When you're ready to plant the full look, start with a mix of weeping brown sedge and hydrangea at the back and on the sides for height. Next, add the amaranthus to the front—the deep burgundy plumes add dramatic color, and the elongated, tassel-like form brings height and depth. We interwove the winterberry throughout the midsection for that pop of red. It's an ideal cultivar for any cooler-weather container due to its compact size and excess of bright berries. This abundant planter, situated at the entry, makes a wonderful first impression for guests as they arrive for Thanksgiving dinner.

PLANTS: *Amaranthus gangeticus* (elephant head amaranth), *Amsonia hubrichtii* (Arkansas bluestar), *Carex flagellifera* (weeping brown sedge), *Coleus* ColorBlaze 'Royale Cherry Brandy' (coleus), *Hydrangea paniculata* 'Bokathirteen' (aka Sweet Summer) (panicle hydrangea), *Ilex verticillata* 'Little Goblin Red' (winterberry), *Parthenocissus quinquefolia* (Virginia creeper), *Pennisetum alopecuroides* 'Lemon Squeeze' (fountain grass), *Asclepias curassavica* (butterfly milkweed)

Purple Majesty

With its aged finish and urn-shaped silhouette, this planter appears as if it were unearthed from the depths of a Grecian hillside. Its plucked-out-of-antiquity look is perfectly juxtaposed by the wildness of the wispy grasses and graceful beauty of delicate fall flowers.

Sweet and elegant, the cranesbill is one of the rare perennials that will perform all summer and well into fall. We've added it in a heaping mound to the front of the planter, with asters filling in on the sides. Asters are a common perennial fall bloomer and a refreshing (while still hardy!) alternative to the prevalent mum. Finally, we planted anise hyssop and little bluestem grass at the back of the planter for height. The little bluestem gets its name for its cerulean hue that shows in spring, but is a fall favorite for its mottled pinkish-purple tips and impressive height come September.

Placing the urn on a plant stand quite literally elevates the entire planting—mimicking a museum-worthy sculpture on a pedestal.

PLANTS: *Aster* 'Double Date Milka' (aster), *Agastache foeniculum* (anise hyssop), *Schizachyrium scoparium* (little bluestem), *Geranium* 'Gerwat' (aka Rozanne) (cranesbill)

Beautiful Boundaries

This pair of planted troughs comes together to capture both an autumnal color palette and the lingering beauty of stretched-out summer, with a rich mix of between-the-season elements. Here we've used apricot-colored coneflower to visually connect one side of the trough to the other. Other elements, like feather reed grass and asters, are repeated throughout to unify the separate containers. Despite the abundance of material packed into this planter, the careful placement of color makes the composition feel playful.

The color palette of rich blacks, burgundies, oranges, and apricots ties everything together. The coral celosia, with its stunning hue, is the true showstopper of the arrangement. We strategically highlighted it by planting the apricot coneflower at its base, creating a triangle of color. Orangey tones are echoed on the ends—on one side with violet, the other side with petchoa, and the dahlia is a visual landing point. The lavender is a foil to accentuate the cool black tones of the bugleweed, 'Dracula' celosia, and ornamental pepper. The stonecrop, Arizona cypress, and feather reed grass create a unifying blue tonality that fills in the spaces between.

PLANTS: *Sedum reflexum* 'Blue Spruce' (stonecrop), *Celosia argentea* var. *plumosa* 'Rainbow Sherbet Mix' (celosia), *Echinacea* 'Fresco Apricot' (coneflower), × *Petchoa* 'Sakpxc021' (aka SuperCal Premium Cinnamon) (petchoa), *Celosia argentea* var. *cristata* 'Dracula' (celosia), *Symphyotrichum nova-belgii* 'Daydream Lavender' (aster), *Ajuga reptans* 'Binblasca' (aka Black Scallop) (bugleweed), *Viola cornuta* 'Pas786643' (aka Sorbet Antique Shades) (horned violet), *Calamagrostis* × *acutiflora* 'Karl Foerster' (feather reed grass), *Cupressus arizonica* var. *glabra* 'Blue Ice' (Arizona cypress), *Celosia argentea* var. *cristata* 'Dragon's Breath' (celosia), *Capsicum annuum* 'Black Pearl' (ornamental pepper), *Dahlia* 'Redhawk Pink Cloud' (dahlia), *Coleus scutellarioides* 'Campfire' (coleus), *Liatris cylindracea* (cylindrical blazing star), *Pycnanthemum californicum* (California mountain mint)

Wild Side

Capture the transition from summer's vibrant energy to autumn's warm embrace with a mix of annuals and perennials, designed to thrive together from high summer to mid-autumn.

Begin the planter in June with leggy, dynamic varieties like 'Midwinter Fire' dogwood—which evolves beautifully through the seasons, from fragrant white flowers in late spring to deep purple blooms in summer, and, finally, glowing orange to red branches in fall—and the striking 'Raspberry Coulis' burnet, another tall variety that lends an overgrown, autumnal charm by October.

Zinnias, stonecrop, and agastache are perfect late-season additions, reaching their peak in fall and providing a vibrant contrast to the earlier plantings. Nemesia, tickseed, and burnet can be incorporated anytime.

This evolving planter is a celebration of seasonal change, bringing new highlights to your garden with each passing month. As a bonus, expect visits from hummingbirds and butterflies—avid fans of zinnias and anise hyssop.

PLANTS: *Agastache foeniculum* (anise hyssop), *Coreopsis* 'Mercury Rising' (tickseed), *Cornus sanguinea* 'Midwinter Fire' (bloodtwig dogwood), *Eryngium ebracteatum* var. *poterioides* (burnet-flowered sea holly), *Persicaria amplexicaulis* 'Fat Domino' (mountain fleece), *Hylotelephium spectabile* 'Autumn Joy' (stonecrop), *Nemesia* 'Innemblora' (aka Sunsatia Blood Orange) (nemesia), *Sanguisorba* 'Raspberry Coulis' (burnet), *Zinnia peruviana* (Peruvian zinnia)

Harvest Hues

Sometimes, the best seasonal planters are the ones that are already planted—you don't always have to start from scratch! Evergreens provide easy four-season interest in any planter; this heavenly bamboo and serviceberry have been living in this planter since spring, and the composition was ready for a seasonal refresh.

Both the heavenly bamboo and the serviceberry boast vivid green foliage and red berries through the fall months, and we wanted to play up that seasonal color with a meadow-inspired understory beneath their branches. We filled in the bulk of the planter's diameter with zinnias and petunias; their bright foliage creates a lively contrast with the vibrant pinks, reds, and purples from all the flower petals. To enhance the confetti-like effect, we sprinkled in the twinspur and echibeckia between the zinnias and petchoas. We added the celosia in a single spot, near the center of the planting but off to one side. Its deep color connects this otherwise bright planting back to its autumnal roots.

PLANTS: *Amelanchier × grandiflora* 'Autumn Brilliance' (serviceberry), *Nandina domestica* (heavenly bamboo), *Celosia argentea* var. *cristata* 'Pas1284114' (aka Concertina Red Dark Leaf) (celosia), × *Petchoa* 'Sakpxc021' (aka SuperCal Premium Cinnamon) (petchoa), *Zinnia elegans* 'Oriole' (zinnia), × *Echibeckia* 'Summerina Orange' (echibeckia), *Diascia barberae* 'Dala Oran' (aka Flirtation Orange) (twinspur)

Wreath Jubilee

Swapping a traditional floral centerpiece with a planted living wreath is an unconventional, elegant way to honor the harvest during gathering season. To create this classic autumn bounty look, we layered on a cornucopia of jewel-toned perennials, seasonal cabbages, and bright succulents. Feel free to experiment—just make sure the specimens have compact root masses.

Plantable wreath forms have large gaps between the wires. To prep the plantable wire wreath form, first line the bottom and sides with the moss to contain the soil. Then plant into the soil and fill the gaps around the plants with more moss.

Next, fill in the wreath plant by plant. Start with the large cabbages first, adding them around the circumference at 12, 3, 6, and 9 o'clock for a sense of symmetry. Add the aeonium and lavender scallops in an asymmetrical form, planting some facing outwards, away from the center of the wreath and others closer to the center, facing inward. Tuck the wintergreen behind the bigger plants for a framing effect. Pansies, heather, and alternanthera fill in the gaps for color and full coverage. Add a lantern or pillar candles in the center of the wreath once the table is set for an extra equinox glow.

To water, fill a large container or sink with room-temperature water and soak the wreath face up for a few minutes. Water often; it will dry out quickly.

PLANTS AND MATERIALS: *Aeonium arboreum* 'Black Rose' (aeonium), *Alternanthera* 'LRU30' (aka Little Ruby) (alternanthera), *Brassica oleracea* 'Osaka White' (ornamental cabbage), *Calluna vulgaris* 'Long White' (heather), *Gaultheria procumbens* (wintergreen), *Kalanchoe fedtschenkoi* (lavender scallops), *Viola* × *wittrockiana* 'Delta Classic Pure Rose' (pansy), *Viola cornuta* 'Black Magic' (pansy), wreath form, sphagnum moss

Harvest Moon

The cornucopia, or "horn of plenty," is believed to have originated in Greek mythology as a never-ending food source for baby Zeus while he was kept in hiding, away from his cruel father, Kronos. Now this gift of abundance is most often associated with Thanksgiving, a holiday defined by its generosity. Our offering celebrates the season's natural bounty—pumpkins and gourds, leafy greens, cabbage—in a low, wide planter that mimics how we'd naturally encounter these same varieties in a garden bed, ready for harvest.

To achieve the seasonal appeal that defines the container, we've planted a mix of clematis, foamy bells, curry plant, alternanthera, and ornamental peppers, each in various stages of their growth cycles. As they settle in, some will end up wilting, creating that spilled-over effect we're after. Feel free to use bolted herbs from the summer herb garden or end-of-season sale plants from your local nursery. Plants that are overgrown and woody will contribute to the overall bountiful, autumnal effect.

The clusters of pumpkins and heads of kale and cabbage play off the planter's roundness, giving a pleasing symmetry to the cohesive whole. And while we've chosen classic autumnal vegetables, the kaleidoscope of heirloom blues, faded grays, and dusty purples gives the planting a cohesive and distinctly nontraditional look.

For pumpkins, the weirder and wartier, the better. Any heirloom varieties available in your area in cool tones of blue, purple, dark green, and black are ideal for this color story. Some good options are 'Jarrahdale', 'Black Futsu', 'Queensland Blue', and 'Blue Doll'. Since pumpkins and gourds rot more quickly when placed directly on damp soil, rest them on terra-cotta saucers nestled between the planted varieties. This way, they stay fresher longer in your display. We also recommend removing the pumpkins when watering or during rain for the same reason.

PLANTS AND MATERIALS: *Alternanthera brasiliana* 'Purple Prince' (alternanthera), *Artemisia californica* (California sagebrush), *Brassica oleracea* (ornamental purple kale), *Brassica oleracea* 'Violet Queen' (ornamental cabbage), *Capsicum annuum* 'Black Pearl' (ornamental pepper), *Clematis terniflora* (sweet autumn clematis), × *Heucherella* 'Autumn Shades' (foamy bells), *Helichrysum italicum* (curry plant), pumpkins

Autumn Spells

Conjure the supernatural with this subtly spooky container. You won't find many traditional Halloween specimens here (nary a burnt orange mum or red cabbage in sight!). Instead, we've chosen plants and flowers in a muted palette of gray, green, and black that capture the bewitching feeling of the holiday with an unconventional twist. We did, however, use a low-profile, ridged planter, reminiscent of a pumpkin's shape, as a subtle nod to the season's more likely star.

Gardeners often forgo petunias in more "elevated" plantings because of their popularity and prevalence, but we're here to change the discourse! Petunias can be used to great effect, adding playfully wobbly height and saturated pops of color—here the deep, velvety midnight hue is perfect for a Halloween-adjacent planting. We centered the kalanchoe to anchor the planting and give it room to shoot straight up as it grows in. Black mondo grass and curry plant act as filler, giving a low cloudlike effect around the rim of the container. We finished off the enchanted planter with a couple craggy branches on one side of the pot for some asymmetry; their organic shape will keep the arrangement from looking too "done."

Start your planting in late summer so the natural rhythms of the seasons transform it into something overgrown, wiry, and lightly worn—the ghosts of high summer still lingering. It should thrive outdoors with relatively little care until first frost.

PLANTS AND MATERIALS: *Hylotelephiuym spectabile* 'Autumn Joy' (stonecrop), *Kalanchoe gastonis-bonnieri* (kalanchoe), *Ophiopogon planiscapus* 'Nigrescens' (black mondo grass), *Petunia* 'Dray68' (aka Black Magic) (petunia), *Helichrysum italicum* (curry plant), foraged branches

Bonfire Nights

In the glow of autumn, this planter blazes with hot colors set against the shifting hues of the season. Fiery blooms and bold foliage stand out beautifully against ornamental grasses, creating a rich, sun-warmed contrast to the fading landscape.

As a bottom "layer" throughout, we've used the perennial orange New Zealand sedge grass, its orange tips complementing the bold pinks and purples within the rest of the planting mix. Bougainvillea, a favored choice in tropical plantings, delivers a potent burst of color. To achieve the lively arrangement, we've deliberately chosen to plant our star, the bougainvillea, on an elevated mound of soil, slightly off-center, and mixed the remaining plants together for a more organic feel.

The undulating curves of the wave-shaped planter provides ample planting space and further reinforces the sense of movement and dynamism within the composition itself. The pedestal serves as a functional element (to raise the planting to eye level) and an aesthetic one (to juxtapose the organic shapes of the planter and planting).

PLANTS: *Aeonium arboreum* 'Black Rose' (aeonium), *Begonia × hiemalis* 'Solenia Apricot' (Rieger begonia), *Bougainvillea × buttiana* 'Rosenka' (bougainvillea), *Carex testacea* 'Prairie Fire' (orange New Zealand sedge), *Gibasis pellucida* (Tahitian bridal veil), *Plectranthus* 'Plepalila' (aka Mona Lavender) (spurflower)

Supercolor Season

More floral arrangement than container garden, this fragrant, saturated stunner is ready to take pride of place at the entry, right in time for a party. We've packed nine flower varieties into this snug planter, using a vibrant fuchsia color palette for pleasing visual cohesion and lime green leaves to add striking contrast.

Color-intense annuals like zinnias and celosia mingle with neon bougainvillea and mango orange verbena in a magenta cluster at one side of the planter. We added lime green Japanese forest grass next to that colorful grouping, giving the eye a spot to rest. Purple perennials like purslane, tuberous verbena, and pansies fill in at the front and back, adding a richness that feels more fall.

The antiqued egg-shaped container is one of the most versatile silhouettes—adding both height and a generous surface area for all the plant varieties. The plants will expire at inconsistent intervals; feel free to pull out dying plants and add new ones—for more on this, see page 281.

PLANTS: *Bougainvillea* × *buttiana* 'Barbara Karst' (bougainvillea), *Celosia argentea* var. *cristata* (celosia), *Hakonechloa macra* 'All Gold' (Japanese forest grass), *Portulaca oleracea* (common purslane), *Verbena rigida* (tuberous verbena), *Verbena* 'Klevp15474' (aka Lascar Mango Orange) (verbena), *Viburnum dentatum* 'Christom' (aka Blue Muffin) (arrowwood viburnum), *Viola* × *wittrockiana* 'Clear Crystals Mix' (pansy), *Zinnia* 'Zesty Purple' (zinnia)

Pollinator's Paradise

The whimsical, unruly features of a cottage garden are often reserved for spring and summer plantings, but we find the romantic, undone look just as charming in fall. In this free-spirited pairing, the weathered texture and aged tones of the containers help anchor the look in autumn, while the pastel colors add an unexpected element for the season.

Positioned in the wider, round planter, the dahlias serve as a central focal point, their blooms rising above the vinca to create height and drama. The petunia, with its profusion of small, bell-shaped flowers in deep purple, adds a dense, colorful mass below. Its trailing habit enhances the layered effect of the arrangement. In the taller planter, a graceful and sprawling butterfly bush shows off arching branches and delicate purple flowers, spilling over the edge of the container to create a relaxed, cascading effect. Two vinca cultivars serve as filler at the base. By keeping the overall color scheme cohesive between the two planters, there's a pleasing asymmetry that feels organic without seeming chaotic. All of these species are pollinator friendly, and the planters will soon be teeming with life.

PLANTS: *Buddleja davidii* 'Pink Delight' (butterfly bush), *Catharanthus* 'Quasar Deep Space Blue' (vinca), *Catharanthus roseus* 'Ocean Black Moon' (annual vinca), *Dahlia* 'Sincerity' (dahlia), *Petunia* × *hybrida* 'Cascadias Autumn Mystery' (petunia)

Pumpkin Craft

As high-summer plantings wilt and their vibrant colors fade, we take pleasure transitioning those almost-dead, just-past-their-prime varieties into fall with the addition of some classically autumnal elements. Anchored by a trio of decoupage pumpkins, this whimsical ode to fall is our unconventional nod to the season's traditional hero.

Pumpkins will always have a place in fall plantings, but we enjoy looking for fresh ways to reinvent this old standby, like decoupaging each one with colorful dried botanicals. By leaving the pumpkins intact, they last longer than their carved or painted relatives.

For the decoupage, we opted for a homemade wheat paste. (To make, simply stir room-temperature water into 3 tablespoons of flour until the mixture is runny and smooth. Add the mixture to ¾ cup/180 ml boiling water and stir until the mixture thickens, about five minutes.) Once you have the paste, apply the mixture on a pumpkin with a paintbrush. Add layers of pressed flowers and leaves in any pattern—have fun and experiment! To prevent rotting, place each pumpkin on top of a terra-cotta saucer nestled in the soil and remove while watering the other plants in the container or during rainstorms.

The textured, tulip-shaped planter, with its built-in pedestal and ample surface area, is perfect for a planting that needs both height and a place to hold pumpkins. We filled in the front third of the planter with false cypress cuttings so that the green would peek out from between the gourds. We added the love-lies-bleeding, coral fountain plant, and bugleweed for their complementary reddish-purple tones, then filled in any remaining space with the dwarf arborvitae, sedum, and butcher's broom grass, each one with varying textures and shades of green. To finish it off, we stuck in ghostwood, winterberry, and serviceberry branches for added height and dynamism.

You may have some of these late-summer blooms in your garden already—great! We also recommend heading to the back of your local garden center and stocking up on all the spent seasonal blooms on sale. Either way, let these shaggy, late-summer stunners do their floppy, fall-is-here thing. Don't fret if your showstopping love-lies-bleeding begins to stretch or the bugleweed starts spilling over the side of the planter. Let each plant go to bed for the season with joyful affect.

PLANTS AND MATERIALS: *Ajuga reptans* 'Purple Brocade' (bugleweed), *Amaranthus caudatus* 'Coral Fountains' (love-lies-bleeding), *Chamaecyparis pisifera* 'Golden Mop' (dwarf false cypress), ghostwood branches, *Ilex verticillata* 'Nciv2' (aka Little Goblin Orange) (winterberry), *Ruscus hypoglossum* (butcher's broom grass), *Russelia equisetiformis* (coral fountain plant or firecracker plant), *Sedum rupestre* 'Angelina' (creeping sedum), serviceberry branches, *Thuja occidentalis* (dwarf varieties) (arborvitae)

Splendor in the Grass

Adding containers to your in-ground gardens gives you so much room to experiment—you don't have to worry about upsetting the surrounding plants and can try out varieties you wouldn't normally place in the garden bed.

This low, wide, fiber cement planter is slightly raised in the center, helping enhance height differences when you place shorter plants in the front and taller plants at the center or in the back. Additionally, the shallow depth is perfect for shallow-rooted plants like succulents and herbs, such as the echeveria, stonecrop, and thyme used here.

To highlight each specimen, we've separated them into five distinct clusters in the pot. Featured at the front, the lavender-hued echeveria's light color helps anchor the planter to its surroundings by echoing the color of nearby garden plants. The lime green cypress adds a shock of bright color and evergreen texture, and the two varieties of stonecrop get spots next on either side of the echeveria, the 'Lime Twister' mimicking the cypress's neon color and the 'Midnight Velvet' adding an autumnal richness. The creeping thyme is gorgeously scented, and its mounding habit creates a cloudlike effect as it grows in.

PLANTS: *Echeveria* 'Purple Pearl' (echeveria), *Sedum* 'Lime Twister' (stonecrop), *Sedum* 'Midnight Velvet' (aka Rock 'N Grow Midnight Velvet) (stonecrop), *Chamaecyparis pisifera* 'Golden Mop' (false cypress), *Thymus × citriodorus* 'Variegata' (variegated lemon thyme), *Calluna vulgaris* 'Beauty Ladies Magda' (heather), *Juncus inflexus* 'Blue Arrows' (blue rush)

Queen of the Autumn Garden

As Pennsylvania horticulturalist and educator Louise Bush-Brown once said, "If the iris is considered the flower of the rainbow, surely the dahlia might be called the flower of the sunset." This sentiment perfectly captures the dahlia's role in painting the garden with the warm, rich hues of autumn, solidifying its status as the true queen of the autumn garden.

Lavish and abundant with deep red dahlias, architectural grasses, and a crowd of annuals, this audacious autumnal planting luxuriates in its bigness. As with so many autumnal plantings, we're celebrating maximalism here—and while no container garden can ever exactly replicate the wild harmony that nature creates on its own, we get close with this vibrant mix of textures, colors, height, and varieties.

To create visual continuity across three separate planters (seen together on the facing page), we've used identical containers and planted both the dahlias and grasses in each. The dahlias are a dramatic focal point, and the tall grasses draw the eye upward and add structure to an otherwise wild planting. The understory repetition of similar plants and colors across the containers creates a rhythmic pattern that guides the viewer's eye from one planter to the next. Mixing broad-leaved plants with fine-textured grasses introduces a tactile contrast that enriches the sensory experience, while the interplay between the soft, rounded shapes of the flowers and the spiky, linear forms of the grasses adds depth and complexity to the design. The use of rich burgundy, deep red, and coppery orange tones creates a cohesive and vibrant color palette that feels quintessentially autumnal.

Identically shaped and sized ceramic containers that show their age individually complement the naturalistic planting style. Find planters with a flat back and rounded front to easily position against a wall or border display.

PLANTS: *Schizachyrium scoparium* (little bluestem), *Dahlia* 'Arabian Night' (dahlia), *Heuchera* 'Plum Pudding' (coralbells), *Celosia argentea* var. *cristata* 'Dragon's Breath' (celosia), *Sedum* Rock 'N Grow series (stonecrop), *Oenothera lindheimeri* 'Kleau04263' (aka Belleza Dark Pink) (gaura), *Coleus scutellarioides* FlameThrower series (coleus), *Amaranthus blitum* (purple amaranth)

Est 1878

Agave Eden

Agave is a mainstay in our store designs and creative photo shoots—they're consistent conversation starters because of their impressive scale and dynamic presence in the garden. And while they're especially beloved in summer for their heat and drought tolerance, they're content to stay outside into the more temperate months of fall, too.

The agave's solidity beautifully contrasts with wispy grasses and stretching perennials, making it an excellent addition to the edge of a late-autumn garden bed. As the garden winds down and autumn continues, the structural agave gets even more space to stand out. It anchors this container with its structure, complementing the botanical elements around it without feeling out of place. Its tough, spiny leaves evoke wild landscapes, while the plant's orderly growth adds a sense of calm.

To reinforce the structure of the agave, instead of underplanting, we topped it with a mix of dark granite rocks collected from forest hikes and bleached white rocks picked up during beach trips. We're big advocates for using these types of foraged collections in containers—not only does it add visual interest, but it also allows for moments of reflection and nostalgia as you enjoy your outdoor spaces.

PLANTS AND MATERIALS: *Agave angustifolia* var. *marginata* 'Variegated Caribbean' (agave), river rocks

First Frost

While the rich sunset tones of late blooms and golden grasses often dominate autumn gardens, there's also room for a more unexpected palette. Cooler hues—such as whites, silvers, and gray-blues—can bring a fresh twist to the fall landscape, providing a serene contrast to the season's fiery colors.

This zinc trough showcases a blend of annuals and perennials, marrying blues and lime greens with crisp white accents. Classic autumn plants like millet, celosia, and coneflower are thoughtfully paired with the more summer-leaning eucalyptus, spurge, lavender, and succulents. We added in airy gaura and knotweed for gentle movement in the fall breeze. The result is a composition that feels both lively and tranquil, proving that autumn's beauty can be as much about subtlety as it is about boldness.

The zinc trough itself adds a modern industrial touch, grounding this rambling, naturalistic arrangement with its sleek, understated style. Troughs work well at entrance points, alongside a gate, or as a resting point for your eye at the end of the drive or walkway.

PLANTS: *Agave lophantha* 'Quadricolor' (century plant), *Celosia argentea* var. *cristata* 'Bkclflm' (aka Kelos Fire Lime) (celosia), *Euphorbia* × *martini* 'Ascot Rainbow' (spurge), *Echinacea* 'Tnechkw' (aka Kismet White) (coneflower), *Eucalyptus cinerea* (silver dollar eucalyptus), *Fuchsia* 'Genii' (fuchsia), *Oenothera lindheimeri* 'Whirling Butterflies' (gaura), *Lavandula* 'Purple Ribbon' (Spanish lavender), *Pennisetum glaucum* 'Jade Princess' (ornamental millet), *Persicaria virginiana* 'Painter's Palette' (variegated knotweed), *Plectranthus forsteri* (Swedish ivy), *Curio talinoides* subsp. *mandraliscae* (blue chalk sticks)

Bright Basketful

Inspired by gathering baskets in the garden, full of just-clipped flowers waiting to be taken indoors and arranged in a vase, this abundant autumn planter is effortless and eye-catching. Its petite size makes it an easy choice anywhere that's needing a color boost, whether it be in a garden corner, on a front step, by an entryway, or against a wall.

We planted the three varieties separately, creating distinct zones of zinnea, Chinese fringe flower, and rose verbena within the planter, to reinforce the idea that they were clipped in bunches from a cutting garden and placed offhandedly in the basket. We added the fringe flower in the back for height, the zinnias in the center, and the rose verbena at the front; the latter is a fast-growing trailer that will quickly cascade over the edge of the planter. This helps soften the edges and naturally integrate the planter into the surrounding landscape. The nontraditional pinks and purples of the plants offer a vibrant contrast to autumnal oranges and browns in the surrounding landscape.

PLANTS: *Zinnia elegans* 'Dark Violet' (zinnia), *Loropetalum chinense* 'Irodori' (aka Jazz Hands Variegated) (Chinese fringe flower), *Glandularia canadensis* (rose verbena or rose vervain)

Still Life

Gourds are not the only autumnal vegetable with an artful appearance. The sturdy, deeply hued eggplant creates a captivating contrast with bright green, gossamer asparagus fern and an airy, neutral trailer like million bells. The finished composition reminds us of a Renaissance still life, especially when planted in an antique urn like we have here.

When planting, start with the eggplants first, as they are the most substantial and the focus of the planter. We've used one 'Fairy Tale' eggplant and one 'Hansel' eggplant, as their compact size and ornamental aesthetic help maintain a balance in the composition. Next, place asparagus fern at uneven intervals from the eggplant. Add white million bells to the front and sides, allowing it to trail over the edge of the planter. Don't pack the plants in—the negative space helps reinforce the overall delicate feeling.

PLANTS: *Solanum melongena* 'Fairy Tale' (eggplant), *Solanum melongena* 'Hansel' (eggplant), *Calibrachoa* 'Can-Can White' (million bells), *Asparagus officinalis* (in fern stage) (asparagus)

Chameleon Fade

This pair of timeworn planters, one slightly larger than its companion, is bountiful with a dense assortment of seasonal favorites, proudly announcing autumn's arrival. Citrus-toned plants brighten up the seriousness of these traditional containers, while the softly faded summer hues mirror the slight patina of the planters. By season's end, these plants will spill gracefully over the container edges, creating a lush, abundant look, which makes them perfect for placing at the entry or edge of the driveway.

We wanted the juicy Little Lime hydrangea, renowned for its zesty blooms, to be the focal point for the larger planter, so we placed it at the front. Behind the hydrangea, we added height with golden millet, a quintessential autumn plant. Bronze fennel, another staple in garden plantings, not only attracts swallowtails but also offers delicate, feathery foliage that softens the composition. Its yellow umbel blooms sway above the arrangement, adding a dynamic, wind-driven element.

The smaller pot is planted with stonecrop and silver tree plant, chosen for their foliar interest and to further reinforce the fading autumnal color story. These two containers are designed to function as a single composition. Positioned side by side, they act as sisters rather than twins: related in palette and plant selection, but not identical. You can use the same plant varieties in each, but allow for variation in positioning and proportion to create a sense of ease and spontaneity.

PLANTS: *Celosia argentea* var. *spicata* 'Sylphid' (wheat celosia), *Coleus scutellarioides* Wizard series (coleus), *Foeniculum vulgare* 'Purpureum (bronze fennel), *Hydrangea paniculata* 'Jane' (aka Little Lime) (panicle hydrangea), *Hylotelephium sieboldii* (October Daphne stonecrop), *Setaria italica* (golden millet), *Pilea spruceana* (silver tree plant)

Gingersnaps

While we've often eschewed the "thriller, spiller, filler" theory in favor of more nuanced planting philosophies (see page 13), it can be fun to find ways to innovate the basics. Here we've applied this classic stratagem across two planters, to full fall effect.

We planted parrot flower alone in the tallest pot, giving space for the plant's bold, upright leaves to stand out as the "thriller" element of the design. This thriller also accentuates the planter's sculptural form and preserves its clean lines. In the smaller container we planted October Daphne stonecrop and coleus as the filler and million bells as the spiller in masses offset from one another so the container feels naturally lush from the start.

Because both planters are terra-cotta and the plants enjoy a complementary color palette, there's a harmony that creates a unified whole across the full composition.

PLANTS: Cabaret Orange Improved *Calibrachoa* 'Balcaborim' (million bells), *Coleus scutellarioides* 'Fancy Feathers Black' (coleus), *Hylotelephium sieboldii* (October Daphne stonecrop), *Strelitzia reginae* (bird-of-paradise)

WINTER

WINTER IS OFTEN CHARACTERIZED by dormancy and minimalism—no flashy blooms or verdant greens to show life. But life is all around even in the coldest months—and winter planters can capture the magical stillness of the season, transforming outdoor spaces into artful displays that complement the crisp air, diffused light, and even a dusting of snow. Winter is also a time to let the containers shine—their individual characteristics on display across the fallow landscape.

Similarly, festive holiday containers can happily celebrate the spirit of the season, adding natural charm to both indoor and outdoor spaces. Holiday containers allow for a seasonal connection to the outdoors, bringing fresh, natural elements into spaces where people gather and celebrate. They echo the themes of renewal and abundance that are central to many holiday traditions, setting the stage for the time for gathering and entertaining.

During this time, more fanciful and dramatic techniques are encouraged, allowing for bold displays of nature's beauty through December. As the holidays pass, these designs can be simplified, pulling back to reflect the restful, serene mood of deep winter. Using natural materials like evergreens, berries, pine cones, and branches keeps the focus on nature's elegance, ensuring your decorations stay connected to the season's quiet beauty.

Using Lighting in Winter Containers

Cozy warm lighting is a hallmark of the season, and at Terrain, we see it as an extension of the design process. Beyond the holidays, subtle lighting plays an essential role, adding warmth and glimmer to short, dark days. Our guideline: Pack away colorful or holiday-shaped/themed lights, but keep soft, warm white lights in play until spring.

Lights can enhance garden structures, uplight ornamental grasses, or highlight the beauty of the containers themselves: The botanicals are the stars of the show during the day, but the slow transition to night as the lights take over is a whole additional element of planter design this time of year. Use lights to emphasize focal points, such as ornamental branches, festive decorations, or the container itself. Wrap lights around structural elements like birch logs, trellises, or tall evergreen stems to add vertical interest. Mix small twinkle lights with larger bulbs for depth and texture. These thoughtful touches extend the season's charm, illuminating spaces with understated elegance long after the festive decorations are gone. Here are a few key considerations.

Types of Lights

LED LIGHTS are energy-efficient, long-lasting, and safe for outdoor use. They won't produce heat, so they are safe around plants. Strings of these lights generally feature flexible wires, so they can wrap around branches, sit under moss, and drape over edges of planters with ease.

BATTERY-OPERATED LIGHTS offer flexibility in placement, ideal for areas without nearby outlets. Their only drawback? Batteries have to get swapped out more often than an LED light or solar panel light.

SOLAR-POWERED LIGHTS are eco-friendly and great for outdoor settings, arriving in either lantern or string form. They charge during the day to illuminate at night.

Styles of Lights

STRING LIGHTS are perfect for wrapping around branches, tucking under decorative toppers, or tracing the arch of a tree's branches. These lights provide a soft, integrated glow that complements the natural form of the planter.

GLOBE LIGHTS, available in clear or vibrant colors, act as bold design accents. They are ideal for enhancing trees with existing structure, serving as ornaments, or adding a base glow to garden arrangements, trellises, or clusters of stems. They're especially striking when wired to spheres or obelisks, offering a playful yet sophisticated light source.

LED WALL-WASHING FLOOD LIGHTS allow for precise color control, dimming, and saturation adjustment. We often use these versatile lights in containers to dramatically uplight individual stems, creating a striking effect that transforms the entire arrangement.

In winter, lighting leads the way. Here we used an outdoor-ready lit branch garland in the branching of the hinoki cypress, echoing the tree's natural structure. The result is a simple yet striking way to highlight the season's evergreens and bring a warm glow to the garden.

Using Fresh Cuts in Winter Containers

Winter is notoriously lacking when it comes to beautiful blooming flowers or bright, delicate greens. Instead, we rely heavily on freshly cut evergreens, foraged branches laden with berries or glossy leaves, and other ephemeral elements. Just like freshly cut flowers, these winter fresh cuts have a short life—a few weeks—when prepped and cared for properly. Below we share some of our best practices for extending their longevity and getting creative with their placements.

1. **Choose long-lasting greens.** Use hardy evergreens like cedar, pine, fir, or boxwood, which retain their color and structure longer. Foliage like eucalyptus, holly, or magnolia leaves can be incorporated for added texture and visual interest, but you should be ready to swap out these varieties more often.
2. **Condition the cuttings.** Trim stems at an angle and immediately place them in water to extend freshness. For added longevity, soak greens between four and eight hours before arranging them in your container.
3. **Anchor the greens securely.** Use soil, sand, or pine nuggets to add weight to containers, helping them resist wind or tipping. Since fresh cuts of greens don't have to be properly planted in a container, you can get creative with how you're anchoring them in the pot.
4. **Layer for fullness.** Once you have established your base of dense evergreens and foliage, layer in branches and specialty greens for contrast and depth. Include cascading greens like cedar or ivy to soften edges and provide movement to the design. Add natural elements like twigs, pine cones, and dried seedpods to connect the planter to its surrounding landscape and ground the planter in its environment. Include festive touches like red berries (e.g., rose hips, holly, or winterberry), shatterproof ornaments, or ribbons to align with the holiday theme.
5. **Protect from harsh conditions.** Place outdoor containers in sheltered spots to protect cuttings from strong winds and heavy snow. Indoors, keep containers away from direct heat sources, like radiators or fireplaces, to prevent drying.
6. **Add moisture.** Regularly mist the greens to keep them hydrated, especially in indoor or dry environments. Colder outdoor temperatures naturally help preserve moisture, but periodic misting can still extend their longevity.
7. **Check regularly.** Inspect for signs of drying or wilting, and replace cuttings as needed to keep the arrangement fresh.

Winter Color Inspiration

In winter's muted landscape, contrast is key. Light and bold accents bring brightness, while varied textures make planters stand out against the subdued tones of the surroundings.

Overnight Frost

Silvery whites, glacial blues, and the cool shimmer of variegated foliage and blue-needled evergreens cast an elegant, ethereal light across the quiet garden.

***Picea pungens* 'Glauca Globosa'** (dwarf globe blue spruce)

Podded eucalyptus stems

***Juniperus horizontalis* 'Monber'** (aka Icee Blue) (creeping juniper)

White birch logs

Helleborus niger (Christmas rose)

***Cedrus atlantica* 'Glauca Pendula'** (weeping blue Atlas cedar)

Eucalyptus stems

***Cupressus arizonica* var. *glabra* 'Blue Ice'** (Arizona cypress)

***Pinus wallichiana* 'Nana'** (Bhutan pine)

Mulled Spice

Evoke the comforting warmth of winter with a grounded palette of rich browns and earthy reds, sparked by vibrant pops of red twigs and berries.

Deciduous magnolia branches

Flame willow branches

Red winterberry branches

Gaultheria procumbens (wintergreen)

Nandina domestica 'Fire Power' (heavenly bamboo)

Dogwood stems

Rose hip stems

Miscanthus sinensis (maiden grass)

Mixed pine cones and pine straw accents

Season's Centerpiece

Designed especially for an effortless transition from fall into winter, this planter feels perfectly at home in the garden as colors change and landscapes shift. We've artfully combined a mix of evergreen boughs, woody plants, and vibrant evergreen foliage for a design that is full of spirited movement and lush density.

Our planted elements here are the leucothoe, Japanese cedar, and creeping juniper. The two latter evergreens will happily continue on in the planter well past the holiday season. You'll need space for the light orb (we use our own brand), so we recommend planting these three close to the back and edges of the container. We placed one slightly off-center for a natural, asymmetrical look. To nestle the orb into the composition, we surrounded it with long-needle pine branches, the longest at the back and sides, with some shorter cuts fanning out at the front of the planter.

Fresh eucalyptus pods provide a whimsical, weighty drape, with just the right amount of elegant flop, and the upright flame willow branches bring a verticality and bold color that help the planter stand out in the daylight.

PLANTS AND MATERIALS:
Cryptomeria japonica 'Black Dragon' (Japanese cedar), *Juniperus horizontalis* 'Blue Chip' (creeping juniper), *Leucothoe fontanesiana* 'Rainbow' (leucothoe), eucalyptus pods, 'Flame' willow branches, long needle pine branches, shore pine boughs, LED branch light

Winterberry Twilight

A nod to crisp winter walks, cozy evenings by the fire, and festive gatherings all at once—our ebullient winterberry planter is a celebration of all we cherish in winter. There's the classic red-and-green color palette, winter branches, and glowy lights, but each with their own surprising (and oh-so-Terrain) twist.

The variegated euonymus is our only planted element here, its cream-and-green leaves bringing a naturalistic brightness to the planter's center that keeps the arrangement dynamic and fresh. The red winterberry branches add striking verticality and a vibrant splash of color that instantly evokes the magic of winter. At the base, a mix of soft, textural, richly hued cuttings of 'Carolina Sapphire' cypress and fragrant balsam fir further reinforce the wintery feeling.

Instead of adding foraged branches and wrapping lights around those branches, we added pre-lit faux branches to the arrangement, carefully weaving them throughout the natural elements to create a lit-from-within glow. For the container, we chose a simple clay pot with a weathered, whitewashed finish. Its neutral, understated look anchors the composition while allowing the plants and lights to take the spotlight.

PLANTS AND MATERIALS: *Euonymus japonicus* 'Silver King' (euonymus), balsam fir branches, 'Carolina Sapphire' Arizona cypress branches, winterberry 'Winter Red' branches, branch lights

Bonsai Light Cascade

This arrangement creates a harmonious balance between simplicity and drama, showcasing the sculptural elegance of nature enhanced by the magic of light. We've highlighted the weeping silhouette of the white pine by under-lighting it with cascading berry-shaped drop lights. The dazzling effect calls to mind the bright beauty of the sprays of yellow flowers on a blooming *Koelreuteria paniculata* (golden rain tree). To under-light any tree, simply follow the natural curves of the branches with the light strand, connecting the strand to the underside of the branch with zip ties or floral wire as you go. Battery-powered lights work best here; you can simply nestle the battery packs at the base of the planter, covering them with pine needles or moss.

As an added decorative element, we created natural ornaments out of fallen pine cones, wiring hooks into the top of each and hanging them off the tree's branches. Each was placed with precision, reinforcing the tree's organic aesthetic and adding depth to the design—don't be afraid to reposition the pine cones and the lights as you work.

A low-profile matte-black planter keeps the focus on the interplay of light and the tree's sculptural beauty. The planter's impressive scale, coming in at 42 inches (106 cm) wide, combined with the tree's 9 feet (15 m) and the glowy lighting, creates an unparalleled display of winter brilliance—a true showstopper in any setting.

PLANTS AND MATERIALS: *Pinus strobus* 'Pendula' (weeping white pine), pine cones, berry-shaped LED outdoor light strand

Midwinter Flame

When the cold days of winter arrive, we seek warmth, whether that's around a fire pit, fireplace, or cozied up indoors. Here we've created a most dramatic sense of that coveted warmth, all thanks to a well-placed LED spotlight nestled in the center of the copse (set on a terra-cotta saucer to prevent the base from getting wet) and the fiery red dogwood branches. These bold branches add dramatic vertical height and vibrant color to the container, creating a striking contrast against the surrounding in-ground natural grasses and subdued winter tones of the garden.

The lush base of eucalyptus foliage softens the structure of the design and adds a cool-toned contrast to the warm reds of the dogwood. As a celebratory bonus, the round leaves look like confetti backlit around the dogwood stems. We added balsam at the bottom to ground the arrangement, providing a layered effect.

MATERIALS: 'Cardinal' red twig dogwood branches, silver dollar eucalyptus branches, balsam fir branches, LED spotlight

Juletrae

The juletrae—the Danish Christmas tree—is far more than just a decoration. It's a deeply rooted symbol of family, warmth, and joy that carries generations of meaning and tradition. In Denmark, the making and decorating of a juletrae is often a collaborative effort, bringing family members together in the spirit of hygge—that special sense of coziness and togetherness that defines the Danish holiday season. There's something profoundly personal about creating your own tree, especially when it's done with intention and love. It becomes a reflection of the hands that made it and the heart that inspired it.

We're drawn to the humble, handmade charm of these trees and admire their simplicity in winter's chill. To differentiate our juletrae from the traditional Christmas tree, we updated our interpretation to mean even the trees themselves are stitched together by hand, a deconstructed "tree" made up of many freshly cut boughs on a tree trunk.

We crafted these outdoor interpretations from balsam boughs, layering each branch onto a birch pole. Starting at the base, we worked our way up, overlapping the branches for fullness and securing them with florist wire. Once the greens were set, we added branch-shaped lights that weave through the foliage, bringing the tree to life with a warm, inviting glow. They're small moments of joy, thoughtfully placed to welcome visitors and bring a little light to the darker days of winter.

MATERIALS: Balsam fir branches, birch pole, lit branch garlands

Dreamlight Cypress

Color-changing lights make decorating a patio tree impactful and simple. The wonderful thing about color-changing-LED technology is that you can set the lights to any color(s) you'd like with the tap of a button. We went for a fiery ombré effect here and, *wow*, is it impressive in the dark winter night!

The golden threadleaf false cypress is known for its open form, and this ultra-lit effect serves to highlight the lacy grace of its branches. To achieve the Technicolor glow, we attached color-changing light strands onto plastic-coated wire branches and then wired those faux branches onto the tree's living ones. It's a time-saver and gives you the flexibility to reuse your lit branches.

Below, soft tufts of ornamental grasses spill over the edge of the container. Autumn moor grass is a cool-season, clump-forming perennial grass known for its fine, arching green leaves with a hint of chartreuse, which add brightness wherever it is used. In late summer to fall, it produces upright spikes of silvery or pale yellow flower heads that mature to a soft beige, providing subtle movement and interest. The structure and color of the grass stays through much of the year, and it provides great scale and movement as an underplanting. Here its feathery texture is illuminated in gentle contrast to the vibrant lights above.

PLANTS AND MATERIALS: *Chamaecyparis pisifera* 'Filifera Aurea' (golden threadleaf false cypress), *Sesleria autumnalis* (autumn moor grass), LED vine lights

Twisted Interest

This planter looks as though it's been caught mid-stretch, its loose limbs sprawling and graceful. With the dynamic asymmetry and free-flowing branching of this design, we hoped to capture the spontaneous beauty that the forest so naturally gives us.

The eastern red cedar is our only planted element, serving as the focal point and foundation of this container. Its natural sprawling habit is the entire point of this planter design, so it's essential to re-create this look. We then wrapped winding contorted filbert branches with LED light strands before sticking them at random points in the planter. Not only do the lights lend a delicate sparkle, but they also help draw the eye out past the planter's edge, as the design so effortlessly breaks beyond its boundaries.

Long rose hip branches come next, adding much needed winter color and even more spindly grace.

The boxy, neutral container anchors all this natural energy with a sense of quiet sophistication. The contrast between the structured base and the free-flowing plant material creates a necessary visual balance.

PLANTS AND MATERIALS: *Juniperus virginiana* 'Grey Owl' (eastern red cedar), foraged rose hip branches, contorted filbert branches, LED light garland

Starlit Spire

While we have included many lush containers that only utilize fresh cuts in this chapter, planting hardy winter-interest plants extends the life of a container planting, offering a refined, low-maintenance option that thrives throughout the season. Our glowing cone design here pairs both weather-appropriate planted varieties with visually interesting nonplanted elements. The simple, sculptural form of the light cone recalls the shape of a living topiary, while its warm, soft glow transforms the design into a living lantern.

At 4 feet (1.2 m) tall, the cone makes a dramatic impact, but without complementary elements, it could feel disconnected from the base. To that end, we planted dwarf juniper and variegated euonymus—both found at a local nursery already perfectly stretched and grown in. The dogwood stems introduce a dynamic, architectural element, bridging the design and tying the centerpiece to the rest of the composition.

A Terrain favorite for their lumpy texture and bright color, Osage oranges are nestled in the planted evergreens to finish off the planting. Often found along the roadside in mid-November in many parts of the country, these vibrant yellow-green spheres bring an unexpected pop of color to the arrangement.

PLANTS AND MATERIALS: *Juniperus procumbens* 'Nana' (dwarf Japanese garden juniper), *Euonymus japonicus* 'Silver King' (euonymus), yellow twig dogwood branches, Osage oranges, lit vine cone

Sky-High Ember Grass

A celebration of winter's resilience and grace, this planter highlights pampas grasses that retain their elegant form and texture even in frost, while the evergreens and eucalyptus offer structure and color throughout the colder months. By day, it's a serene addition to the landscape, and by night, it's pure enchantment—an illuminated reminder of the beauty that winter brings.

The tall, airy plumes of pampas grass rise like soft golden wands, their feathery texture catching both the wind and the light. Once night falls, the real magic begins: A warm white LED spotlight from below ignites the grasses, accentuating their delicacy and color. The light seems to breathe life into them, creating a soft, ethereal glow that turns the ordinary into the extraordinary.

Below the planted grasses, the silvery green tones of fresh-cut eucalyptus offer a calming contrast, their rounded leaves forming a smooth, velvety layer that ties the design together. The fresh-cut cedar spilling over the edge adds a rich foundation that grounds the planter, balancing the brightness and height of the grasses with deep green hues and hardy texture. Both fresh-cut varieties can simply be stuck into the dirt by the branch.

The clean, minimalist lines and dark, neutral tone of the metal box container let the natural beauty of the plants take center stage while providing a modern edge. Together, the grasses, eucalyptus, and evergreens create a stunning juxtaposition of textures and tones—airy and soft, vibrant and moody, all working in harmony.

PLANTS AND MATERIALS: *Panicum virgatum* 'Heavy Metal' (switchgrass), pampas grass, silver dollar eucalyptus branches, western red cedar branches, LED spotlight

Forest Lantern

Only three elements, and not a single fresh cut or blooming flower. Sometimes—and especially in winter—a container design comes alive without anything living at all. Here we've wrapped a metal orb in preserved sheet moss, breathing "fresh" life into its hard frame. To achieve this, we cut sheets of the sheet moss into strips the same width as our orb's lines. We attached these strips to the orb with light-colored string, but you could also wrap the moss with floral wire at intervals.

The layered string lights set the entire thing aglow, highlighting the organic curves of the orb for an effortlessly enchanting design. While it shines brightly during the holidays, this design transitions beautifully to an all-season statement maker, beckoning loved ones inside with its soft warm glow on cold winter nights. To elevate the design even further, try hanging one (or a few) from the branches of a nearby tree.

MATERIALS: Metal orb, sheet moss, LED light strands

Radiant Bramble

The humble tumbleweed, most often associated with arid landscapes and rugged wilderness, can be transformed into something elegant and boisterous when adorned with lights. Their intricate, wiry structure creates a unique and organic silhouette that glows beautifully when lit, making them an unusual focal point for winter.

You can readily find dried tumbleweeds from dried floral sellers online. Of course, you can always hunt for a tumbleweed in the hot summer months and keep it close by until winter rolls if you have the forager's spirit. The practicality of a tumbleweed planting for winter is obvious—it's already dried, it's hardy, and if weather reaches it, its wild structure won't betray any signs of wear. Adding a delicate strand of microlights creates a floating, ethereal effect. We've gone conceptual with this one and omitted a planter altogether to let the tumbleweed's natural shape and texture shine. If you'd like to use a container, we suggest settling your bramble into a whitewashed planter to enhance its rustic lightness. To keep it in place, weight it down with stones at the base—the light strand's battery pack will also work as an anchor.

PLANTS AND MATERIALS: *Salsola tragus* (prickly Russian thistle), twining LED light strand

Winter Frost

Evergreen foliage, foraged branches, dried natural elements, and zinc leaf accents in frosty tones of white, beige, gray, blues, and greens come together in a design that's more naturalistic sculpture than living planting.

We gathered dried hydrangea and switchgrass from the garden, a mix of fresh evergreens from the forest, and birch branches from a nearby tree. You can purchase the dried elements and birch branches from your local craft store and can often find fresh-cut evergreen branches from the hardware store or local Christmas tree vendor (cuttings from your own holiday decorations work, too!).

We filled the container with soil and added chicken wire to the top of the soil, bending it down the sides a little to hold in place. You don't see it once the elements are added to the planter, but the wire provides necessary structure for the cut branches and other plant matter. The black spruce tip and Fraser fir give height in the back, mugo pine adds bright color toward the edges, and the grasses wind through the midsection. We placed the three-dimensional hydrangea heads front and center, with a trio zinc of leaves fanning out on either side.

MATERIALS: Black spruce branches, Fraser fir branches, mugo pine branches, switchgrass stems, dried hydrangea, birch branches, metal stems

Harvesting Holiday

You've trimmed the tree and decked the halls—and now you've got a fragrant heap of fresh-cut evergreen boughs and berry branches waiting to be transformed into something completely new and original. For us, that means creating a layered understory for a potted black spruce tree. Add a light strand and a pair of glowing LED pine cones and our here-and-there spruce feels wholly holiday.

Central to our planting is a slender black spruce tip, a favorite choice for holiday containers for its festive fragrance and seasonal charm. Its sparse, natural form evokes the simplicity of a Nordic forest—minimalist, understated, and authentic.

To create the understory, we started with a base of fresh-cut Fraser fir branches, but any evergreens would work here. Layer them loosely around the trunk of the tree, creating a wreath shape as you go. You can push the ends of the branches into the soil near the trunk to keep them in place, or you can secure them together using floral wire. Next, we wove a few juniper berry and rose hip branches into the greenery base for pops of color. The last botanical elements are a few cedar boughs tucked under the "wreath" so that their branches drape over the sides of the planter.

We nestled a pair of LED pine cones in the center of our "wreath," but you can add cones from your own backyard! We topped it all off with a few light strands, lighting both the tree itself and the wreath form.

MATERIALS: Western red cedar branches, rose hip branches, black spruce tips, pine cones, Fraser fir branches, juniper berry branches, LED pine cones, LED vine lights

Zen Conifer

Ah, a peaceful respite from the hurried hustle and bustle of the holidays. We've forgone the festive trimmings, baubles, and color here for a sophisticated Zen garden–inspired design that reminds us to slow down and savor the season's simple beauty.

The dwarf weeping eastern hemlock, with its feathery fronds and bonsai-like branching, lends itself well to the quiet drama we're going for here. As a collector's conifer, the 'Pendula' cultivar can be somewhat difficult to track down. Any other well-shaped evergreen with airy foliage or open forms—like Japanese maples, dwarf conifers, or similar evergreens—would work beautifully, too.

The subtle illumination the string lights provide enhances the natural structure of the tree, giving it a radiant glow from within and transforming it into a living piece of sculpture. To enhance the Zen garden feel, we added a mound of smooth river rocks at the base. They also provide a nice visual weight, anchoring the tree and giving a harmonious balance between the tree, lights, and the planter itself—a white fiber cement container that perfectly complements the tree and lighting without competing for attention.

Whether placed in a quiet garden corner, on a patio, or as part of a series of illuminated pots lining a walkway, this design creates an enchanting, calming effect on its admirers.

PLANTS AND MATERIALS:
Tsuga canadensis 'Pendula' (dwarf weeping eastern hemlock), LED light strand, river rocks

Enchanted Alpine Garden

This miniature winter wilderness captures the imagination and invites exploration. It's almost as if you could simply step onto the slate "pavers" and enter into the magical garden on your own. With its textural contrasts, layered elements, and naturalistic details, it's a loose interpretation of a classic alpine garden.

The curated scale of the elements—larger stones and conifers paired with tiny moss mounds and slate pieces—gives the container the feeling of a living diorama. It's bound to be a conversation piece! We've positioned ours right on the patio so passers-by can fully appreciate its fanciful, fairy-tale-like qualities.

To achieve the captivating intrigue of this little landscape, start with uneven soil to create hills and valleys. We placed the Atlas cedar at the "top" of our planting to serve as the focal point. Its silvery needles bring a frosty, wintery tone to the arrangement, evoking high-altitude landscapes. The smaller conifers "below" add depth and create a sense of scale. A variety of lush, velvety mosses cover the soil, mimicking the forest floor and adding soft contrast to the spiky texture of the conifers.

Adding berried wintergreen branches and mini lights brings this container directly into the magical vernacular of festive holiday time, but the use of hardy conifers and natural materials ensures it can remain enchanting year-round.

PLANTS AND MATERIALS: *Erica tetralix* f. *alba* 'Alba Mollis' (cross-leaved heath), *Erica × darleyensis* f. *aureifolia* 'Mary Helen' (heather), *Calluna vulgaris* 'Firefly' (heather), *Cedrus atlantica* 'Sapphire Nymph' (Atlas cedar), *Chamaecyparis obtusa* 'Just Dandy' (hinoki cypress), *Gaultheria procumbens* (wintergreen), *Hypnum imponens* (sheet moss), *Juniperus communis* (common juniper), *Juniperus procumbens* 'Nana' (dwarf Japanese garden juniper), *Leucobryum glaucum* (cushion moss), *Thuja occidentalis* 'Islprim' (aka Primo) (arborvitae), slate shards, LED spotlights, LED light strands

Glowing Sentinel

Snowy, glowy, and oh so cozy—our magical hinoki lights up even the darkest nights. Set against a backdrop of stone walls and snow-covered ground, this glowing tree feels like a beacon of warmth and celebration. Hinoki cypresses are favored for their deep, woodsy fragrance, meandering horizontal branching, and broad, pyramidical silhouette. Hinoki can happily grow in planters, as long as the pots are large enough to accommodate their deep root system and have a proper drainage hole. Of course, any potted evergreen will do for this design, but the more mature the trees are, the bigger the impact they'll make.

We started at the top of the tree with a light garland that's shaped like tree branches, laying the garland's tendrils on top of the tree's branches and securing them with floral wire. We draped a second garland down the tree's trunk, once again starting at the top and letting the lights cascade to the planter below. The effect is a fully illuminated tree when really, the effort was minimal to work the existing lit vine over the branches, instead of weaving lights onto every branch of the tree individually. The last step, of course, is the snow—not something we can conjure on demand, unfortunately, but when the flakes do begin to fall, oh, what magic it is!

PLANTS AND MATERIALS: *Chamaecyparis obtusa* (hinoki cypress), lit branch garlands

Welcome Light

We have a deep affinity for collector conifers, particularly miniature and dwarf varieties. These smaller-scale, slower-growing specimens combine intricate beauty with a sense of refinement. And we love keeping them in containers, styled with a bonsai-inspired aesthetic that complements the clean, simple spaces in our gardens.

We wanted to enhance the natural charm of this pine, which resides in a planter year-round, without overshadowing its inherent elegance. Instead of decorating it with ornaments and turning it into a mini Christmas tree, we chose to highlight its unique qualities in a subtler way. We added a strand of G40 globe lights as the planting's "topper," forgoing the more traditional moss or stones for this glowing alternative. To keep the lights upright and neatly arranged, we used an easy yet clever trick: landscape staples. The effect is stunning, especially at night as the strand uplights the tree, casting a gentle glow and offering an understated yet undeniably special welcome.

PLANTS AND MATERIALS: *Pinus cembra* 'Westerstede' (Swiss stone pine), LED globe light strand with reflectors

Seeing the Light

A tangle of illuminated, twisting branches rise as a burst of light out of this exuberant planting. Their fluid, organic shape suggests movement, almost as if they've been swept by a winter wind, and the warm golden light they emit adds a sense of whimsy and enchantment. Underneath, a cozy mix of beloved winter berries and branches. The overall effect? Glowy, showy, and oh so inviting.

The wind grass and coralbells are our two planted elements—bringing feathery texture and rich color respectively. We placed them in the center of the container, leaving plenty of room at the edges for the fresh-cut elements. Both offer year-round interest and so can remain the base for countless design iterations once these fresh cuts have faded.

A mix of fluffy juniper branches and wispy 'Caroline Sapphire' cypress bunches form clusters at the edges, the juniper berries an almost exact color match to the weathered planter below. Orange winterberry branches add a flash of vivid color and craggy lichen-covered branches bring a naturalistic feel. A few foraged pine cones (we painted ours white with acrylic paint) are nestled in the center, hidden if not for a closer look. Finally, the tree branches, wrapped in a warm white light strand, ensure you can enjoy the planter through the long winter nights.

MATERIALS: Coralbells, juniper branches, 'Carolina Sapphire' Arizona cypress branches, orange winterberry branches, lichen-covered branches, white-painted pine cones, wind grass, foraged tree branch, LED light strand

Tranquil Blue Hues

Monochromatic doesn't have to mean monotonous, and these blue Christmas-inspired planters prove a single-color scheme can feel fresh and unexpected. The captivating blue tones of the plants pair perfectly with the blue-gray of the planter, taking the monochromatic look to the next level.

Planter pairings should be sisters, not twins—don't feel as though they have to be identical to work in tandem with each other. To that end, we planted a slim, unsheared Sargent cypress in only one of the pots, to act as the statement piece. We underplanted both with 'Blue Star' juniper, its bushy habit echoing the rounded gray-blue planter. Cut eucalyptus stems, short and tightly arranged at the base of the planters, form a dense, velvety ground layer. For a festive finish, we cut vibrant red dogwood stems short and added them to the tree planter, which pop playfully against the cool tones and add a hint of holiday cheer.

PLANTS AND MATERIALS: *Cypress sargentii* (Sargent cypress), *Juniperus squamata* 'Blue Star' (flaky juniper), naked seeded eucalyptus branches, cardinal dogwood branches

Rustic Radiance

Transform your winter garden with planters that double as lanterns, beckoning guests indoors. Boxwood topiaries clipped into flawless spheres or cones are a perfect canvas for LED string lights. Gently pressing the lights into the foliage creates a subtle, ethereal glow from within, avoiding the harshness of visible strings and adding depth to the design. Find basket planters suited for indoor and outdoor use—they often arrive with a plastic liner that can be removed for watering. The woven materiality and natural colors help create that cozy, homey feeling the living lantern needs. We finished off the planting with humble pine straw for extra texture and earthy tonality.

PLANTS AND MATERIALS: *Buxus sinica* var. *insularis* 'Franklin's Gem' (Korean boxwood), pine straw, LED light strand

Timeless Winter Greens

Resilient evergreens like the hard-wearing boxwood are, of course, a safe choice for cold-weather containers. Adaptable, drought tolerant, deer resistant, hardy, and low maintenance, they're a proven winner for winter months—but that doesn't mean they have to be boring. Sometimes, a simple nod to the season is enough, whether you're looking to brighten up a garden corner or accent a walkway, and this boxwood-cedar pairing brings subtle winter appeal with minimal effort.

We've kept the petite boxwood trimmed into a tidy sphere and stuck cedar clippings around the edge, allowing them to flutter over the rim of the planter, where the boxwood's glossy, deep-green foliage plays off the cedar trimmings' roughened texture and washed color. An egg-shaped planter enhances all the rounded shapes from the plant matter and a simple string of LED lights lets them continue to shine once the sun goes down.

PLANTS AND MATERIALS: *Buxus sinica* var. *insularis* 'Rlh-Bi' (aka NewGen Liberty Belle) (Korean boxwood), western red cedar trimmings, incense cedar trimmings, LED light strands

Winter Blossom

Festive fun—it's the reason for the season! While we'll always enjoy creating sophisticated, elegant designs for the winter holidays, sometimes the merriest planters are a little playful.

For this arrangement, we started with the *Pinus strobus* 'Ground Hugger', a low-growing weeping pine with softly curving boughs that create a loose, organic shape. Planted in a ginger jar–shaped container, it looks relaxed yet full of personality. We added spongy, lush reindeer moss as the underplanting to create a cohesive all-green look as a base for the shining lights.

The retro starburst light reflectors elevate this look into something super special. These mid-century stunners add so much charm, contrasting beautifully with the feathery texture of the pine. It's joyful and nostalgic without veering into kitsch. We nestled this planter along the sidewalk, where its soft glow offers a delightful surprise to passersby.

PLANTS AND MATERIALS: *Pinus strobus* 'Ground Hugger' (eastern white pine), reindeer moss, starburst light refectors

Tiny Trees

Miniature conifers' understated beauty shines during winter, offering an unexpected range of colors, textures, and forms to work with in an otherwise muted season. From soft blue tones to golden highlights and rich, deep greens, these evergreens pack far more variety than most people expect. Our goal with this design is to create a miniature forest, so density is key.

Unlike spring or summer container designs, where plants grow in and fill out as the season progresses, winter containers need to look full and lush right from the start, as they won't have the benefit of rapid growth. This is why we added a whopping seven different conifer varieties to this modestly sized container. A compact cloud of 'Ryoko-gyoku' Japanese cedar sits directly in the center, with golden hinoki cypress and dwarf mountain pine filling in around it. A branch of feathery deodar cedar peeks out from under 'Amber Gold' arborvitae at the front, and Lawson's cypress adds height at the back, with 'Blue Arrow' juniper nearby.

The variety helps enhance the natural diorama feel, as does the addition of a couple driftwood branches, winterberry branches, and some planted mondo grass that trails over the side of the pot.

PLANTS AND MATERIALS:
Chamaecyparis lawsoniana 'Ellwoodii' (Lawson's cypress), *Chamaecyparis obtusa* 'Crippsii' (golden hinoki cypress), *Cedrus deodara* (deodar cedar), *Cryptomeria japonica* 'Ryoko-gyoku' (Japanese cedar), *Gaultheria procumbens* (wintergreen), *Juniperus scopulorum* 'Blue Arrow' (Rocky Mountain juniper), *Ophiopogon planiscapus* 'Nigrescens' (black mondo grass), *Pinus mugo* 'Gnom' (dwarf mountain pine), *Thuja occidentalis* 'Amber Gold' aka 'Jantar' (arborvitae), driftwood, winterberry branches

Evergreen Orb

A vine-covered sphere wrapped in lights becomes a dominant feature of any container design, particularly at night. This element is especially effective in winter containers, taking up visual mass while creating stunning impact when paired with greens. It's a simple, prefabricated solution you can easily build around, perfect for anyone who loves bold style with a low-maintenance vibe. You can find pre-lit vine spheres at Terrain, or make your own using a dried vine sphere and a string of lights from your local nursery or craft store.

This planter has a stripped-back brilliance: a no-fuss florist bucket, a glowing vine sphere, some fragrant balsam, and a touch of English ivy. The reddish stems of the ivy tie in with the twig orb, creating subtle cohesion that feels unforced but oh so intentional. It's casual, it's cool, and it's proof that you don't need over-the-top frills to make a statement. While we almost always insist on a planter with a drainage hole for outdoor winter planters, we don't have to worry about that here since there are no true planted elements. Simply arrange the fresh cuts the same way you would a flower arrangement and nestle the lit vine sphere at one side. And if you don't have a florist bucket, any vase, crock, planter, or basket will work here.

Whether it's by the front door, perched on a step, or at the foyer, this planter delivers serious winter charm.

MATERIALS: English ivy vines, balsam fir branches, lit vine orb

Nested Evergreen

We'll never tire of glimpsing the glowing presence of an evergreen-nestled sphere near the garden's edge. This handwoven wicker globe leans on the naturally wonky eucalyptus and western red cedar branches for its visual interest—wrap a few twinkly fairy lights around it and you've got an enchanting sculptural garden form. The arrangement achieves balance with the solid upright presence of the sphere countered by the horizontal spill of evergreens.

Eucalyptus is a seasonal favorite for its fragrance, shape, and longevity. We've added three different types here—silver dollar, naked seeded, and silver bell—to really show off the plant's varying tones and shapes. Their soft, muted shades, ranging from silvery blue-green to dusty green, is a lovely complement to the bright cedar branches that form the structural integrity of the base itself. These fresh cuts retain their beauty even as they dry, making this planter a durable option to last through the holiday season and into January.

MATERIALS: Wicker sphere, LED light strand, silver dollar eucalyptus branches, naked seeded eucalyptus branches, silver bell podded eucalyptus, western red cedar branches

Greenspires

Tall, narrow conifers rise confidently from the centers of this planting pair like little green spires stretching for the sky. Their reach gives the design its height and formal presence, while their vibrant green color draws the eye upward, creating a sense of calm and symmetry that makes these planters ideal for framing a doorway or a path or for highlighting a cozy garden corner.

Though the conifers may be the first element that captures your attention, the magic happens at the base. Cascading layers of incense cedar spill over the edges of the containers, softening the lines and imbuing the arrangement with a sense of lush abundance. The variety of greens, from bright chartreuse to silvery blue, gives the planters depth, almost as if they were plucked straight from the heart of the forest. Pine cones help break up the sea of green, and their chunky texture feels wonderfully tactile. The planters' earthiness anchors the arrangements without stealing the show, and the subtle nest of pine straw around the base ties everything together, blending the planters seamlessly into the garden setting. These containers aren't flashy—they don't need to be. Their charm lies in their simplicity and their connection to nature.

PLANTS AND MATERIALS: *Ophiopogon japonicus* (mondo grass), *Osmanthus heterophyllus* 'Goshiki' (variegated false holly), *Thuja occidentalis* 'Smaragd' (aka Emerald Green) (arborvitae), incense cedar branches, 'Carolina Sapphire' Arizona cypress branches, Osage oranges, sugar pine cones

Golden Dogwood Glow

Traditional holiday planter designs often feature a mix of cold-tolerant annuals and perennials, evergreens, and English ivy—and for good reason. Not only are these plants hardy and weather tolerant, they also bring a bounty of texture, color, and seasonal interest to an otherwise sparse time of year for gardens. This luminous dogwood design uses many of these classic elements within a timeless urn shape but introduces a few fresh design choices to make it more dynamic and engaging.

There are only two planted elements to this container—the ornamental cabbage and the English ivy. To make room for the branches and lighting element, we planted the frilly, flowery cabbage at the front and sides of the planter, and interspersed the ivy around the edges to encourage trailing. Then, we simply placed a battery-powered LED spotlight into the center of the planter (you can set it on a terra-cotta saucer to stop it from settling too far down into the soil) and arranged the yellow dogwood branches in a circular pattern around it. The yellow tones of the branches pick up and reinforce the golden glow from the light. To really capture and reflect the light, don't be afraid to create a dramatic cluster—here we used about twenty-five sticks.

Bunches of 'Carolina Sapphire' Arizona cypress act as a topper for the container. Their cool, blue-green hue contrasts perfectly with the warm yellows and whites, grounding the arrangement in a winter-inspired palette. All told, this planter brings seasonal texture and interest to the garden no matter the time of day, but once the sun sets, it acts as a beacon welcoming guests and bringing warmth to long winter nights.

PLANTS AND MATERIALS: *Brassica oleracea* 'Nagoya White' (ornamental cabbage), *Hedera helix* (English ivy), 'Carolina Sapphire' Arizona cypress branches, yellow twig dogwood branches, LED spotlight

Atlas Urn

Perched atop a classic pedestal, this weathered urn serves as a perfect stage for a spirited holiday arrangement, blending its own traditional structure with the festive exuberance of the branches and plants. It's a planter that radiates seasonal warmth and good cheer—all with subtle hints to the holidays.

We chose a planter with a wide diameter (48 inches/ 122 cm across) to give room to the oversized metal orb—the star of the show. Indeed, our glowing celestial body anchors the entire design with its grand size and soft illumination. To create a bright beacon of your own, you can always use zip ties to fasten a light strand to any structure (a trellis or obelisk would also work here).

We've situated a mix of four evergreens both directly inside the orb (but slightly off-center) and right outside it. The 'Grey Owl' juniper adds a feathery texture, the 'Silver King' euonymus a glossy shine, the cypress a gnarled, twisting silhouette, and the 'Blue Star' juniper a mounding habit. Once we planted the evergreens, we added striking red winterberry stems to play into the holiday feel. A few willow branches add enthusiastic height and dimension, their linear structure mimicking the orb's radiating light. Pine straw at the base softens the transition from the urn to the plantings, creating an organic grounding layer that enhances the arrangement's landscape-like quality.

PLANTS AND MATERIALS: *Juniperus virginiana* 'Grey Owl' (eastern red cedar), *Juniperus squamata* 'Blue Star' (flaky juniper), *Euonymus japonicus* 'Silver King' (euonymus), *Cypress sargentii* (Sargent cypress), 'Flame' willow branches, red winterberry branches, pine straw topper, G40 Stargazer light strand

Frosted Grace

This planter's intricate latticework and weathered patina brings classic garden elegance, mostly reserved for summer or fall, straight into winter. The pedestal base elevates the arrangement, drawing the eye upward and making it a striking focal point. While perfect for formal gardens, the planter's refined design also offers a beautiful contrast within wilder, more naturalistic settings.

For this design, only a flower worthy of being placed on a pedestal would do, so we chose the exquisite winter-blooming 'Buttermint' camellia, a hardy variety down to Zone 6. Camellias are exceptional in the winter landscape, offering glossy evergreen foliage that holds its beauty year-round. When its delicate blooms emerge in late winter, they symbolize resilience and hope, a quiet promise that spring is just around the corner.

To support our star, we've added a layer of cushion moss atop the planter, creating a rich landscape of texture. For an alternative underplanting, hellebores would also make a lovely choice, with their evergreen foliage and winter flowers offering a similarly welcome gift to the garden. Sheet moss, used as a liner within the latticework, not only holds the soil in place but also adds an organic element that complements the planter's timeless charm.

This combination of structure, evergreen beauty, and winter blooms creates a design that celebrates both the starkness and quiet hope of the colder months, bringing life and elegance to the darkest time of year.

PLANTS: *Camellia* 'Buttermint' (camellia), *Hypnum imponens* (sheet moss), *Leucobryum glaucum* (cushion moss)

Little Berries

The hellebore is one of our favorite harbingers of spring—a resilient early bloomer that brings a beacon of light to the darker months. This petite pot is packed with these sweet beauties, among some silvery fresh cuts to ground it in winter's palette. It's a hopeful, lovely little planter that's big on charm.

With four plant varieties packed into this small planter, we've kept the color palette restrained, all washed neutrals and silvery blues. The nodding hellebores act as glowing lanterns, while the silvery cushion bush and blue juniper berries play off each other, shimmering like frost in the low winter light. The wintergreen berries add an ever-so-slight pop of pastel pink, warming up the cool tones. Because this is such a bright, bushy, vertical planting with no trailers, we chose a statement planter that's an integral part of the overall design, its white cast picking up the tones of the vibrant hellebore petals.

PLANTS AND MATERIALS: *Helleborus niger* (Christmas rose), *Gaultheria procumbens* 'Winter Fiesta' (wintergreen), *Calocephalus brownii* (cushion bush), berried blue juniper branches

CONTAINER PLANTING BASICS

We're thrilled you've picked up this book to (we hope) find a fresh source of inspiration as you plan your next container design—no matter where you are in your gardening journey. And with that inspiration, we also hope you've gotten more than few practical tips along the way. Below we've complied even more useful guidelines, advice, and instruction to make sure you're set up for a healthy, thriving design in every container.

Choosing Your Plants

Before diving into specific planting ideas, it's important to consider three essential factors that guide any successful design: plant hardiness zones, sun conditions, and aesthetic intent. In this section, we'll focus on the first two—your zone determines what will survive, and your light conditions shape what will thrive. Both are foundational to any container or garden composition. As for aesthetics, we introduced our principles for the visual language of planting at the beginning of this book (see page 13), and we encourage you to revisit them as you plan. Together, these three elements ensure your design is successful, enduring, and inspired.

UNDERSTANDING HARDINESS ZONES (AND WHEN TO BEND THE RULES)

Plant hardiness zones—determined by the USDA—are based on the average annual minimum winter temperature. They help you understand what plants can typically survive outdoors, particularly in the coldest months. Once you know your zone, it becomes much easier to choose plants that are well suited to your climate. Most local nurseries stock selections that thrive in your region, so you're often halfway there without even trying.

That said, a zone rating tells you what to expect, not what's possible. Container gardening lives outside many of the rules of in-ground planting: Planters can be moved, sheltered, or even brought indoors, but they also expose roots to greater temperature extremes, particularly in winter, since they lack the insulating buffer of the surrounding soil. So while a plant labeled hardy to your zone might survive in the ground, it may need extra protection in a pot.

This is where annuals truly shine. Designed to deliver a single season of abundant growth and bold color, annuals don't need to survive winter, so there's no pressure for them to conform to zone ratings. Their job is to perform spectacularly, then bow out gracefully, leaving you with a clean slate to reimagine your containers next year. For many designers, this freedom is part of the thrill: a new palette, a new structure, a new story—season after season.

Beyond broad geographical grow zones, it's also worth considering the concept of microclimates when choosing plants for container gardens. A microclimate can mean anything from how your outdoor spaces are situated topographically to how many large trees are in your area, how much wind exposure your space gets, and the overall protection from the elements your space receives. All these factors—both individually and combined—can make for variable conditions across a single property.

At Terrain, we enjoy experimenting with these variables, so we might plant something that's rated for a slightly higher grow zone in a container or garden that happens to be in a warmer, more protected area of our stores or homes. As a way to get started with this kind of experiment, identify a portion of your property near your house, perhaps that's on a side that feels more protected from the elements. Often these spaces are under trees and close to structures where the plants might obtain some benefit from radiant heat, or under eaves that protect from the worst of ice or snowfall. You can increase your chances of success by "mulching in" your containers with extra mulch or mulched leaves at the end of a season, basically giving them an added layer of insulation (for more on overwintering, see page 281). It's also worth paying specific attention to the watering needs for these spaces, as by nature of their being protected, they will often naturally get less rainwater, so they might require supplemental watering (for more on watering, see page 280).

The bottom line: Let your zone inform your choices, but don't let it constrain your creativity. Container planting is part horticulture, part theater—and you're allowed to dream a little.

SUN REQUIREMENTS

Of course, the best thing you can do for a container is place the pot in a spot that gets the correct amount of sun for the plants inside it. That said, there are other factors to consider, whether your only option is less-than-ideal light conditions or you're trying to learn what works best and where.

General Tips

- **Observe your space.** Take note of how sunlight moves through the area during the day. Maybe a spot gets the perfect dappled sun for six hours a day, but the remaining two are quite harsh. Maybe a shady tree nearby could help protect the planter in the harsh afternoon heat, or perhaps a patio umbrella could do the trick.
- **Group by needs.** Place containers with similar sun and water requirements together for easier care. This is especially helpful if you are traveling and will have someone coming over to tend to your plants while you're away—or if you have folks in your family who don't have as established a green thumb as you do.
- **Make them work for you.** The beauty of a garden not in the ground is that you can move it whenever you'd like to! If you are looking to spruce up transitional spaces or rooms with changing light conditions, simply move your containers when you need to.
- **Be flexible.** Some plants, like begonias or geraniums, can tolerate both sun and shade, so if you're looking for true versatility in your plants, seek out those that are most adaptable to varying light conditions.

When Planting in Sun

- **Provide adequate water.** Sun exposure can dry soil quickly, so water frequently to keep plants hydrated, especially in hot weather.
- **Protect from intense heat.** In extreme heat, consider adding temporary shade during the hottest part of the day or grouping containers to reduce evaporation.
- **Select heat-tolerant varieties.** Opt for plants that thrive in high heat, like lavender, lantana, or tickseed, for consistent performance. Because full sun intensifies evaporation, choose plants with drought tolerance, and use larger containers that retain moisture better.

When Planting in Shade

- **Consider light levels.** Not all shade is created equal. Understand the type you're dealing with—dappled, partial, or deep—and match plants accordingly.
- **Avoid overwatering.** Shaded areas retain moisture longer, so reduce watering frequency to prevent root rot.
- **Enhance soil drainage.** Use well-draining soil mixes to ensure water doesn't accumulate in shaded spots.
- **Brighten the space.** Select plants with light or variegated foliage, like angel wings or coralbells, to add contrast and prevent the area from feeling too dark.

Choosing a Planter

There are two main considerations to keep in mind when choosing a planter: practicality and aesthetics—in that order. Your practical needs will vary with each planter type, design, season, and location. Is this a succulent and cacti design in an extra-sunny spot in the middle of July? An oversize moisture-regulating, heat-absorbing terra-cotta container might be the move. Alternatively, if you're looking to create a charming centerpiece for the Thanksgiving table, a teak boat (with no drainage!) will be the best option. Once your practical needs are met, you can experiment with color, texture, and ornamental variations. While always aesthetically interesting, each planter shape is also suited to different plant types. Some containers offer ample surface area for shallow roots, and others are substantial and tall for deep-rooted specimens. Here we're sharing the most easily accessible and helpful containers to have in the garden.

Jar

These egg- or barrel-shaped planters share many of the same characteristics of taper planters, though because of their rounded silhouetted and ample curves, they offer a much more casual, relaxed silhouette. Most jar planters have a generous surface area and hold a lot of soil volume, which is perfect for container designs that invite a plethora of plant varieties into a single planter.

Urn

Elegant and refined, urns are an elevated planter option. Because of their shape, most cannot hold much soil and have a shallow depth, so we prefer to use them for shallow-rooted plants that don't require a lot of water. That said, while the impulse may be to pair an urn planter with more sophisticated plant varieties, we love how these cultivated silhouettes look with wild, prairie-inspired plantings.

Taper

Perhaps the most popular and ubiquitous—the taper arrives in a myriad of sizes, styles, and materials, each one defined by sloping sides.

Trough

Another small-scale planter ideal for a tabletop or mantel, trough planters share a lot of qualities with their bowl counterparts. Because of their straight sides, they're also fun to "connect" down the length of a table for a dinner party and can be easily repurposed to new homes once the event is over.

Bowl

It's our favorite as the vessel for a tabletop centerpiece due to its shallow depth and decorative shape. Whether you've chosen a rustic piece of driftwood for an outdoor summer barbecue or a sweet wire basket bowl for an Easter brunch, bowl planters are perfect for of-the-moment plantings that are meant to be admired in the round.

Straight-Sided

Thanks to their ample soil volume and surfacearea, straight-sided planters are a wonderful choice for growing larger specimens over the course of a long time span. We prefer these statement-making containers for trees (swapping out underplantings to flow with the seasons).

Jar

Trough

Urn

Bowl

Taper

Straight-Sided

Preparing a Container

Before the fun can begin, the foundation must be laid. Prepping a container correctly helps ensure your plants' longevity—which is the goal after all your hard work!

1. Check that the container has drainage holes. If it does not, you can easily drill holes through most outdoor container materials; holes help prevent rot and ensure proper drainage. If the container is too fragile or difficult to drill, fill the base with extra drainage medium (see step 2) or leave the plants in the grower's pots so you can easily remove to water.
2. Fill one-quarter of the planter with pine nuggets or mulch bark to provide drainage, aeration, and moisture control. For exceptionally large or heavy planters, filling in the bottom one-quarter reduces the weight once soil is in.
3. Add peat-free potting mix to fill to about 2 inches (5 cm) from the container's edge. (Peat-free potting mix is mixed with perlite, vermiculite, or pine bark. This light, sterile mix gives the nutrition, water retention, and drainage properties required of many popular container plants. See the note at right for more on peat.)
4. Remove plants from grower's pots by gently pressing on all sides of the plastic so the soil begins to loosen from the sides. Tip the pot so the plant can fall into your hand. Gently shake out excess soil and tease apart roots if they're matted. Begin adding plants to the container, positioning so the top of every root ball is level with the soil surface.
5. Once all plants are positioned, backfill with soil so the roots are fully covered and the soil is level with the planter's edge.
6. Water thoroughly. Soil may settle and compact after watering; check in on your planter about an hour after watering and top off with more soil if necessary.
7. Add toppers or underplanting. (For a more in-depth look at toppers and underplantings, see opposite.)

A NOTE ON SUSTAINABILITY

Consider sustainability when choosing a growing medium. There is an ongoing and complicated global conversation around peat; while some countries are making headway toward sustainable peat farming, peat is a natural resource and peat mining contributes significantly to global CO_2 emission levels. Coconut coir is readily available as a by-product of coconut farming, but there are concerns around the ecological impact of its processing, which requires large amounts of water. Innovators are pioneering peat- and coir-free potting mixes that prioritize sustainability, so look for options with these factors in mind while the industry works toward sustainable solutions.

Toppers and Underplantings

A topper is a decorative, typically nonliving material placed on the surface of the soil in a container. It enhances the aesthetic appeal while serving practical purposes like protecting the soil from erosion, deterring pests, and insulating roots. Some common toppers are outlined below.

An underplanting involves living plants added beneath or around the primary feature plant in a container. These plants interact with the main planting by filling gaps, creating layers, and softening transitions between the container and its surroundings. Underplantings contribute to the overall vibrancy of the arrangement, offering complementary textures, colors, and sometimes seasonal interest.

River Rocks: Use tumbled stones to add pleasing, natural texture to substantially sized plantings. River rocks can also be mixed into a fine gravel topper as accents.

Bark Mulch: Small bark mulch and small bark nuggets are great options for a natural setting. We like to use them with tropical understory plants, like ferns.

Moss: Sheet or clump moss makes for a lush, highly textured understory for small trees or plants with long, slender stems.

Slate Shards: Lay pieces of slate flat atop the soil for a solid, smoky backdrop with a low profile—ideal for showcasing vines, creeping plants, or succulents.

Small, Colorful Gravel: Accentuate a color story and draw attention to plants with unique silhouettes or hues by adding a layer of small, colorful gravel on top of the soil.

Pine Straw: Pine straw or pine needles are great natural toppers any time of year, but especially in early spring, fall, and winter months. The pine needles naturally tangle together, offering an effective soil cover.

Container Maintenance and Seasonal Evolution

For thoughtfully planted containers to truly thrive through a season, they often require subtle interventions and updates that respect the plantings' natural rhythms while extending their beauty and vitality.

WATERING TIPS

By taking the time to understand your container plants' needs and responding to the conditions around them, you can ensure they stay vibrant and healthy throughout the seasons.

- **Check soil moisture regularly.** Use your finger to feel about an inch or two (2.5 to 5 cm) below the surface. If it feels dry, it's time to water. If you can't get your finger through the gorgeous toppers on your pot, we suggest using a moisture meter, which is a probe that goes into the soil and provide a reading on its moisture level. When you do water, do so deeply, ensuring that moisture reaches the entire root zone. Stop once water begins to drain from the bottom of the container to keep from oversaturating the soil.
- **Water in the morning.** This gives plants a chance to absorb moisture before the heat of the day. This also minimizes evaporation and keeps leaves dry, reducing the risk of disease. Overwatering is a common pitfall, so let the soil dry out slightly between waterings and ensure your containers have proper drainage to avoid water pooling at the bottom.
- **Prep your containers with moisture in mind.** Weather plays a significant role in how often you'll need to water. Hot, dry days may require daily watering, while cooler or rainy conditions will allow you to cut back. Adding a layer of mulch, gravel, or moss on top of the soil can help retain moisture and reduce evaporation, keeping your plants hydrated for longer.
- **Think about the container type.** Pots with adequate drainage holes are a must, and materials like terra-cotta may dry out faster, requiring more frequent watering. Grouping plants with similar water needs in the same container is another way to streamline your care routine and keep all your plants thriving.
- **Adjust your watering habits as the seasons change.** Plants typically need less water during cooler months and more during active growth periods. You'll still want to water in fall and winter occasionally, though, to support plant health.

FEEDING YOUR PLANTER

From organic brews to synthetic blends, fertilizer choices abound—and the "right" one often depends on your expectations for the season. Whether you're aiming for lush foliage, abundant blooms, or simply maintaining healthy structure, the key is understanding your plants' needs and tailoring your approach. Whether you opt for an organic or chemical fertilizer, it will be labeled with a set of three numbers known as an NPK value. These numbers express the percentage by volume of nitrogen (N), phosphorus (P), and potassium (K) in the mixture. Generally speaking, nitrogen promotes leafy, green growth, phosphorus encourages root strength and flowering, and potassium builds overall plant health and resilience. Local nurseries are a gold mine of advice, and a bit of research goes a long way. A combination of slow-release and liquid fertilizers offers both a steady nutritional foundation and flexible support throughout the season.

Start with Slow-Release Fertilizer

When planting, mix slow-release pellets directly into your soil. These coated granules break down gradually, feeding for 60 to 120 days. For flower-heavy displays, choose a formula labeled for blooms—often higher in phosphorus.

Supplement with Liquid Feed

As your plants grow, offer additional support with water-soluble fertilizer. Mixed into your watering routine, this type of fertilizer gives roots an easy-to-access boost. A balanced formula (like a 10-10-10 NPK value) is a good, all-purpose option. Again, consider a formula with elevated phosphorus levels (e.g., 5-10-5 NPK) if you wish to encourage flowering.

Use Foliar Sprays for Quick Recovery

For midseason stress—during heat waves or dry spells, or after heavy pruning—foliar feeding can revive tired plants. Spray a liquid fertilizer directly onto leaf surfaces (both top and underside), where nutrients are rapidly absorbed—be sure to check the instructions on your product for the suggested dilution ratio. Apply foliar sprays in early morning or evening to prevent sunburn. We personally swear by a fish emulsion foliar spray during peak summer growth. It's effective, but yes—it smells exactly like you'd expect. Apply it at dusk, when the neighbors are indoors and the scent can fade overnight.

DEADHEADING

Deadheading encourages a plant to redirect valuable energy to producing new blooms, while keeping your containers looking their best. Regularly monitor flowering annuals and perennials in your containers for spent blooms, and remove either by hand or with a clean pair of snips or scissors. This can be especially important for annuals after heavy rains. We're always finding pockets of spent blooms that are ready for deadheading as we walk through our gardens, both at home and in our stores!

EXTENDING THE LIFE OF YOUR PLANTER

As we suggest throughout the book, swapping out season-specific or spent plants from an otherwise healthy container is a great way to extend the life of your design and evolve the overall look across the seasons. You can utilize a sharp trowel to slice into the soil around the root ball of the plant you want to remove, taking care to isolate its foliage from the plants you are leaving in the planting. To fit additional plants into a crowded planter, a bulb planter is a great way to quickly hollow out targeted planting space, expanding the hole to the necessary size with multiple adjacent cuts.

OVERWINTERING

If you are in a climate that gets a seasonal frost or freeze, you might want to take extra precautions with any less-hardy container plantings. Plants in containers are more readily exposed to potentially damaging freezes because their roots will likely experience temperatures closer to the outside air temperature (those planted in ground are typically more insulated). Depending on your resources and space, this can be achieved by grouping many containers together to help insulate them, moving containers to a more sheltered place outdoors, "mulching in" your containers (adding a thick, insulating layer of mulch around and on top of the container), or even bringing planted containers into an unheated basement or garage for winter. (Many times a combination of these approaches is used.) Containers should be watered deeply at the end of the growing season and prior to the first freeze, and outside of regular weather events, should not be watered while dormant.

ACKNOWLEDGMENTS

As we celebrate the natural world through the pages of this book, we are reminded that our individual endeavors are often the result of collective efforts. We would like to thank all the folks whose tireless passion is at the heart of Terrain.

To our agent, Judy Linden at Stonesong, and publisher Lia Ronnen and editor Bridget Monroe Itkin at Artisan, your unwavering support and patience have been invaluable in shaping the stories behind our books. Thank you also to the rest of the Artisan team, including Ivy McFadden, Paula Brisco, Becky Terhune, Suet Chong, Elissa Santos, Hillary Leary, Donna Brown, and Zach Greenwald.

To the incredibly dedicated and resourceful group that led this book from concept to reality: Beth Smith, Ashley Fossile, Sarah Dill, Megan Parry, Ed Brogna, Justin Speers, Christian Loos, Jennifer Jones, Brianne Jamison, Taylor Engels, Magen Krones, Jenna Hornby, Cynthia Coslett, Erika Boal, Melissa Lowrie, Matt Poarch, and Allison Willey, and to our talented design teams, who supported the project creatively.

Greg and Melissa wish to share their heartfelt gratitude with our friends and family, whose support, patience, and encouragement sustained and inspired us throughout the years and while creating this book. A special thanks to Jay Lassiter, Sarah A. Hyde, Kristin Lehmkuhl, Adam Leach, Simon Leach, and Jean Bartley.

To our Terrain family, including Richard and Meg Hayne, Wendy McDevitt, Tricia Smith, Dave Zeil, and Beth Smith, thanks for your generous support and guidance over the past eighteen years. And to all those whose excellence and dedication has fostered our growth every day—all our store, buying, merchandising, visual, creative, Design by Terrain, web, marketing, photo, planning, and allocation teams, we are incredibly grateful for your talent, hard work, and inspiration.

This incredible team, both past and present, has shaped all that we are and have done, including this special book.

Thank you—we couldn't have done it without you.

Thank you also to the designers who contributed to the following containers:

Stephanie Alba and Sharon Ferguson: Orchid Odyssey (page 132), Broad Strokes (page 57), Not-So-Traditional Topiary (page 70)

Jean Bartley: Forest Lantern (page 229), Juletrae (page 217), Frosted Grace (page 268)

Leslie Drinkwater: Celestial Succulents (page 92), Reaching New Heights (page 78), Morning Mist (page 74), Hidden Gem (page 58)

Lori Foester and Lydia Reichardt: Shade Seeker (page 54), Made in the Shade (page 62)

Jenna Hornby: Winter Frost (page 233)

Matthew Muscarella, Sophie Ruggio, and Dana Velazquez: The Gathered Palette (page 81), Garden Alcove (page 73), A Classic Contrast (page 45)

Roots Fine Gardening: Far Afield (page 95)

PHOTOGRAPHY CREDITS

All images courtesy of Martha Lawlor except for the following:

Greg Lehmkuhl: Pages 4–5; 12–13; 15 (left and right); 17; 20; 21; 31, 31, 30; 31; 32; 33; 34; 36; 37; 38; 39; 42; 43; 52; 53; 64; 65; 68; 82–83; 87 (bottom right), 88–89; 91; 96; 97; 99; 104; 105; 106; 107; 110; 112; 117; 120; 122; 123; 126; 127; 136; 137; 138; 139; 140–141; 144; 145; 146; 147; 149; 153; 154; 156; 157; 162; 164; 165; 171; 181; 182–183; 190; 194; 197; 201; 210; 212; 213; 218; 219; 240; 241; 264–265; 266; 267; 277 (top left, top right, bottom left); and 282.

GAP Photos: Pages 28 (top left, top center, top right, middle left, middle center, middle right, bottom left, bottom center); 29 (top left, top center, top right, middle left, middle center, bottom left, bottom center, bottom right); 84; 85 (top left, top right, bottom center, bottom right); 86 (top center, top right, middle left, middle center, bottom center, bottom right); 87 (middle left, middle center, middle right, bottom left, bottom center); 142; 143 (middle right, bottom left, bottom center, bottom right); 204 (top left, top right, middle center, middle right, bottom left, bottom center, bottom right); and 205 (middle left, middle center, middle right, bottom left, bottom center).

Isa Salazar: Pages 204 (top center, middle left) and 205 (top left, top center, top right, bottom right).

Jebulon, CC0, via Wikimedia Commons: Page 215.

INDEX

NOTE: Page numbers in *italics* refer to photos.

Melissa Bartley is the visual director at Terrain, where she shapes the brand's creative experience through immersive, seasonally inspired environments. Drawing from experience across garden, home, and film design, she brings narrative vision and a gardener's sensibility to her work. She cultivates spaces where wildness meets intention, ideas take root, and home connects organically with nature.

Greg Lehmkuhl is the creative director at Terrain, where he leads product innovation with a seasonal, globally inspired approach. Growing up in a gardening family, he developed a lifelong love of container gardening, particularly for greening challenging spaces. His passion spans every season, from creating temporary showcases to crafting perennial combinations that evolve beautifully over time.

TERRAIN, a home and garden lifestyle brand under the URBN brand family, was founded in 2008 on the site of a hundred-year-old nursery in Glen Mills, Pennsylvania. The brand has now grown to include nine stores across the country, with more stores to come. Terrain has been featured on *Today* and CBS's *Sunday Morning*, as well as in *The New York Times*, *The Wall Street Journal*, *Vanity Fair*, *Vogue*, *Martha Stewart Living*, *Elle Decor*, and *InStyle*. Their first book, *Terrain: Ideas and Inspiration for the Decorating the Home and Garden*, was published in 2018, followed by their second, *Terrain: The Houseplant Book*, in 2022.